the Psalms a complex and sealed book searched out and outlined

TWO PLOTS AGAINST THE LORD

the Psalms a complex and sealed book searched out and outlined

TWO PLOTS AGAINST THE LORD

ORIE A. MILLER

Pleasant Word
A Division of WINEPRESS PUBLISHING

Printed in the United States of America

Packaged by Pleasant Word, a division of WinePress Publishing, PO Box 428, Enumclaw, WA 98022. The views expressed or implied in this work do not necessarily reflect those of Pleasant Word, a division of WinePress Publishing. Ultimate design, content, and editorial accuracy of this work are the responsibilities of the author.

ISBN 1-57921-694-3
Library of Congress Catalog Card Number: 2003106654

This book is dedicated in loving memory to my wife,

Sarah E. Miller, MD
1912–2001

Contents

Introduction 9

Chapter 1: A Prophetic Book 19
Chapter 2: A Sealed Book 37
Chapter 3: A Complex Book 49
Chapter 4: A Distorted Book 55
Chapter 5: A Similar Book 73
Chapter 6: A Hallelujah Book 87

Bibliography Bibles 101

Introduction

The book of the Psalms, which is the longest book in the Scriptures, is a prophetic account of the Lord's first and second coming. The Psalms open with the authorities in Israel rejecting their future king whom God sent to become the savior of men. The book ends with a lengthy account of the Lord's return when Israel will accept Him as their Savior and King.

The prophets who authored these psalms wrote what the Spirit of God spoke through them about the Lord, for He alone knows the thoughts of God. What the Spirit spoke through David about the Lord in Psalms 3–30 was written about one thousand years before the Lord fulfilled what was penned in them. But what David wrote in these psalms, about the Lord's sufferings, death, resurrection and ascension, was a hidden matter, for the death of Christ was a mystery, which God kept hidden for ages (Rom. 16:25).

What the psalm writers wrote concerning the Lord's coming as King, prior to and following it, remains to be fulfilled. These are the unfulfilled psalms: 2, 9 and 33–150. Approximately 3000 years have passed since most of them were written, but they will soon begin to be fulfilled.

The complex arrangement of the Psalms into five books by the Spirit is a mystery to the commentators as is the organizing theme that ties these five books together. Because this book is not understood, it previously has never been outlined.

For several centuries B.C., the Jews called this five-book arrangement of the Psalms The Little Books of Moses. But the Jews left no record of the likeness of the five books of the Psalms to the five books of the Law. Their likeness is presented in Chapter 5.

Genesis	Psalms 1–41
Exodus	Psalms 42–72
Leviticus	Psalms 73–89
Numbers	Psalms 90–106
Deuteronomy	Psalms 107–150

PSALMS 1 AND 2

The title of this Book, *Two Plots Against The Lord*, is based upon the first verses of Psalms 1 and 2. What God concealed in Psalm 1:1, John made known that it was the Sanhedrin that plotted to take the Lord's life (John 11:45–53). God, in His secret wisdom, kept hidden what He destined for our glory before time began, for if the rulers of this age had understood it, they would not have crucified the Lord of Glory (1 Cor. 2:6–8). Psalms 1 and 2 serve as an outline for the entire Psalm collection.

Psalm 2 is an introduction to the largest portion of the Psalms. It speaks openly about the plot of the kings of the nations, who plan to destroy the Lord on the day He is to return to Zion as King. But the Lord destroys them. This destruction of the nations is presented in Psalm 9 of Book 1, Psalms 60–64 of Book 2, Psalms 75–83 of Book 3 and Psalms 90–91 of Book 4. And the psalms that follow these accounts in Books 2–4, as well as all of Book 5, describe various aspects of the Lord's reign as King.

During the long night of the Day of Atonement, that immediately follows the Great Tribulation, the wrath of God and the Lamb will be poured out upon the raging nations that looted and plundered Israel. And every Israelite who calls upon the Lord and makes

Him his refuge will be spared and protected. He will see the punishment of the wicked as 1000 fall at his side and 10,000 at his right hand. But no harm or disaster will come near his tent, for the Lord will command His angels to guard him. Because he loves Me, says the Lord, I will rescue him; I will protect him, for he acknowledges My name. He will call upon Me, and I will answer him; I will be with him in trouble. I will deliver him and honor him. With long life I will satisfy him and show him My salvation (Isa. 17:12–14; Ps. 91:5–16).

As the Lord comes from heaven in the morning of the Day of Atonement, He will send His angels with a loud trumpet call, and they will gather His elect from the four winds, from one end of the heavens to the other (Matt. 24:30–31). He will bring you to the land that belonged to your fathers, and you will take possession of it. He will make you more prosperous and numerous than your fathers. The Lord your God will circumcise your hearts and the hearts of your descendants, so that you may love Him with all your heart and with all your soul, and live (Deut. 30:5–6).

With deep compassion, He will bring them back to dispossessed nations and to settle them in their desolate cities. As their Redeemer, He has sworn not to be angry with them, and never to rebuke them again. He said, I will build you with stones of turquoise, your foundations with sapphires. I will make your battlements of rubies, your gates of sparkling jewels, and all you walls of precious stones. All your sons will be taught by the LORD and great will be your children's peace. He also said, In righteousness you will be established; tyranny will be far from you; you will have nothing to fear. Terror will be far removed; it will not come near you. . . . No weapon formed against you will prevail, and you will refute every tongue that accuses you. This is the heritage of the servants of the LORD (Isa. 54:7–17).

To Israel the Lord has said, Arise, shine, for your light has come and the glory of the Lord rises upon you. . . . Nations will come to your light, and kings to the brightness of your dawn. . . . To you the riches of the nations will come. Herds of camels will cover your land, young camels from Midian and Ephah. And all from

Sheba will come bearing gold and incense and proclaiming the praise of the Lord . . .

Your gates will always stand open, they will never be shut, day or night, so that men may bring you the wealth of the nations. . . . I will make you the everlasting pride and joy of all generations. . . . Your sun will never set again, and your moon will wane no more; the Lord will be your everlasting light, and your days of sorrow will end. . . . The least of you will become a thousand, the smallest a mighty nation. I am the Lord; in its time I will do this swiftly (Isa. 60:1–22).

A HIDDEN MATTER

Although the Psalms present a prophetic account of the death and resurrection of the Lord, His coming to die was a hidden matter. Although God chose us in Christ before the creation of the world and predestined us to be adopted as His sons through Jesus Christ, His will was not made known; His will concerning us and His Son was a mystery. God has made known the mystery of His will, which He purposed in Christ, to be put into effect when the times have reached their fulfillment. He then will bring all things in heaven and on earth together under one head, even Christ (Eph. 1:4–10).

God chose us in Christ that we might be for the praise of His glory. He marked us with His seal, the Holy Spirit, as a deposit guaranteeing our inheritance until the redemption of those who are His possession (Eph. 1:11–14). As for the riches of our glorious inheritance, after the Lord displays the exceeding greatness of His power in our resurrection, God will place all things under His feet and appoint Him head over everything for the Church, which is His body (Eph. 1:18–23).

To the Ephesians the apostle Paul said, “In reading this, then, you will be able understand my insight into the mystery of Christ, which was not made known to men of other generations as it has been revealed by the Spirit to God’s holy apostles and prophets. This mystery is that through the gospel the Gentiles are heirs together with Israel, members together of one body, and sharers together in the promise in Christ Jesus" (Eph. 3:2–6).

Christ was a mystery until the church age began, and, what the Holy Spirit spoke through David in Book I of the Psalms, concerning the Lord's death and resurrection, God kept hidden from the Jews until the Spirit had come and revealed it to the holy apostles and prophets. The Jews never understood that the lamb they annually killed and ate, as they observed the Passover, was a type of the Lamb of God they would kill on a future Passover day. They neither believed the Lord's testimony that the Father sent Him, nor did they believe His many miraculous signs that testified to this fact (John 5:36–40).

As the Lord's time to die drew near, He asked His disciples, Who do people say the Son of Man is? They replied, Some say, John the Baptist; others say, Elijah; and others, Jeremiah or one of the prophets. But Jesus asked, Who do you say I am? Simon Peter answered, You are the Christ, the Son of the living God. Then He warned His disciples not to tell anyone that He was the Christ (Matt. 16:13–20).

Following this, He announced to them three times that He must go to Jerusalem and suffer many things at the hands of the elders, chief priests and teachers of the Law, and that He must be killed and on the third day be raised to life (Matt. 16:21; 17:22–23; 20:17–19). But they did not understand any of this. Its meaning was hidden from them, and they did not know what He was talking about (Luke 18:34).

After He was arrested on His appointed day to die, He was taken to the court of the high priest where many were observing the Passover night by watching. Many were strutting about to find false witnesses against Him that they might kill Him. Finally, the high priest said to Him a second time, Tell us if You are the Christ, the Son of the Blessed One? I am, said Jesus. And you will see the Son of Man sitting at the right hand of the Mighty One and coming on the clouds of heaven. The high priest tore his clothes and asked the crowd, You have heard the blasphemy. What do you think? They all condemned Him as worthy of death (Mark 14:61–

64). According to the Law, the blasphemer was to be stoned (Lev. 24:14).

John referred to this rejection of the Lord when he said, He was in the world, and though the world was made through Him, the world did not recognize Him. He came to that which was His own, but His own did not receive Him (John 1:10–11). Because God hid from the Jews what was written about Him in the Psalms, it was necessary for Jesus, in the evening following His resurrection, to open the minds of the eleven and others with them, so they could understand what was written in the Scriptures about Him (Luke 24:44–47).

If the Lord needed to open the minds of His disciples to understand the Psalms, it was necessary to ask Him to do the same for me. He complied. When the Lord as King teaches all in Israel, they will say to Him, Open my eyes that I may see wonderful things in your Law (Ps. 119:18). He will also fulfill their request.

THE NEW TESTAMENT SAINTS

It was from His cross that Jesus began to speak of those who believed in Him when He said, As for the saints who are in the land, they are the glorious ones in whom is all My delight (Ps. 16:3). And after His death, He looked forward to the day when we are assembled with Him in the presence of God. To those assembled, God will say, May your hearts live forever (Ps. 22:26).

And at the Kings marriage to His royal Bride, He promises to make her sons princes in all the earth (Ps. 45:9, 16–17). This will be fulfilled when God places all things under the Lord's feet and appoints Him head over everything for the Church. He then will subdue the nations under our feet (Eph. 1:22–23; Ps. 47:3).

Also, before He and His glorified saints leave the beautiful city of God in the sides of the north, the Lord will say to them, Walk about Zion, go around her, count her towers, consider well her ramparts, view her citadels, that you may tell of them to the next generation. For this God is our God forever and ever;

He will be our guide even to the end (Ps. 48:1–3; 12–14). During their reign on the earth, His glorified saints must describe to successive generations this city and tell them about God who makes it secure forever. When the kingdom age ends, this earth will be destroyed and a new heaven and a new earth will be made. Then the city of God will come down upon the new earth and God will dwell with men. He and the Lamb will be the light of it and those who were kings, who ruled with Him on earth, will bring their splendor into it (Rev. 21:1–24).

A BLESSED BOOK

The Psalm collection may well be called A Blessed Book. It has been such to many in centuries past. According to the NKJV, the word *bless* and its varied forms appear eighty-four times in the Psalms. This is more often than in any other book in the Bible. Just as the word *blessed* begins the first line of Psalm 1:1, so also the word *blessed* begins the last line of Psalm 2. The man referred to in each of these two psalms represents two different peoples upon whom the Lord will bestow His blessings.

In Psalm 1:1, the blessed man is not a partner with the wicked council that took counsel against the Lord. Instead, he takes delight in the Lord's Word and meditates upon it day and night. He bears fruit for the Lord in his season, and the Lord causes him to prosper in whatever he does. Eventually he will stand in the presence of God, in the assembly of the righteous. These righteous ones will assemble in Gods presence before the kings of the nations assemble against the Lord in Psalm 2.

The blessed man in Psalm 2:12 is typical of him who takes refuge in the Lord at the time He is destroying the nations assembled against Him. After the destruction of the wicked, the Lord will return to Zion and all who took refuge in Him, in the time of His wrath, will also return to the land of Israel. A second blessing is pronounced upon such in Psalm 3:8. In the seventy-five psalms that speak of the Lord's reign as King, blessings are pronounced by Him and His people fifty-seven times. According to the NKJV, the Lord blesses His people thirty times and they bless Him twenty-seven times. The kingdom age will be a blessed time for Him and His people.

PURPOSE

It was the Lord's purpose, after He arose from the dead, to have His disciples understand that He was alive. For three days they mourned and wept. He enabled them to understand that He fulfilled what was written about Him in the Psalms and He desired that they preach repentance and forgiveness of sins in His name to all nations, beginning at Jerusalem. He clothed them with power from on high to bear witness of His salvation (Luke 24:46–49).

Likewise, it is the desire of this writer to enable the psalm reader to recognize and to proclaim what is written about the Lord in Psalms 3–30. Psalms 3–22 speak of His suffering, Psalms 23–28 tell of His three days in the grave and Psalms 29–30 proclaim his resurrection and ascension. Much of what is written in these psalms is found in no other place in the Scriptures. The Psalms will enrich the ministry of anyone who uses them to proclaim the price the Lord paid for our salvation.

Also, the purpose of this writer is to enable the psalm reader to understand the unfulfilled portion of this Book. This portion begins with Psalm 33 and covers the last seven years of this age, which is divided in the middle of these years (Dan. 9:27). The outline provided for the five Books at the end of chapter 2 identifies the psalms that speak of each half of the seven years. The numerous events that are to take place or begin to take place in the middle of these seven years are presented in Daniel 11:29–12:3. After the last three of these events are presented, Daniel was told to close up and seal the words of the scroll until the time of the end (Dan. 12:4). Also, after the Lord spoke about the last half of the seven years, Daniel did not understand. To him the Lord said, Go your way, Daniel, because the words are closed up and sealed until the time of the end. Many [at that time] will be purified, made spotless and refined, but the wicked will continue to be wicked. None of the wicked will understand, but those who are wise will understand (Dan. 12:9–10).

The outline of the five books identifies the psalms that speak of the destruction of the nations immediately after the Great Tribulation. This destruction takes place during a darkness of unknown length of the Day of Atonement. In the morning of this day, the Lord returns to earth as the King of Israel. The purpose for this book, with its outlines and comments, is to enable the reader to understand what he is reading, regardless if he is reading about the fulfillment of the first plot against the Lord, about the events that take place between the two plots as well as what takes place following the final plot.

The first three chapters following this introduction give reasons why the Psalms have not been understood. Chapter 4 explains what men have done to the Psalms that added to the difficulty of understanding them. Chapter 5 presents the likeness of each book of the Psalms to the five books of the Law, respectively. And the last chapter, which tells of the Lord's return to Zion, presents in order the peoples who appear before Him to express their praises to Him for what He has done for them. The praises to the Creator by those He created and by what He created will never end.

My strong desire to understand the Psalms has been a long and difficult project. It was costly, but rewarding. God has said, Though it cost all you have, get understanding. Esteem her, and she will exalt you; embrace her, and she will honor you. She will set a garland of grace on your head and present you with a crown of splendor (Prov. 4:5–9). This reward is for whoever will pay the price.

Chapter 1

A Prophetic Book

The Psalms, as a prophetic book, open with the longest and most detailed account in the Scriptures of the Lord's final days on earth as a Prophet. No one understood these prophecies about the Lord until He had fulfilled what was written about Him. No Jew, not even the Lord's apostles, understood these prophecies that speak of His suffering and resurrection until the day He arose from the dead. In the evening of that day, He informed them that He had fulfilled what was written about Him in the Psalms and He opened their minds to understand the Scriptures (Luke 24:36–49).

The Sanhedrin did not know that Psalm 1:1 spoke of them. They also did not know who Jesus was or what was said about Him by the prophets, which were read every Sabbath in their places of worship. So they carried out their plot to take the Lord's life and fulfilled what was written about Him (Acts 13:27–31). Also, because the present day commentators do not search out what God concealed in Psalm 1:1, they do not know how the story about the Lord in this book begins, and neither do they who read their comments.

John makes it known in his gospel that following the plot by the Sanhedrin to take the Lord's life, Jesus flees Jerusalem with His disciples, to the town of Ephraim near the desert (John 11:45–57). What the Lord said at this place, where His sufferings begin, is given in Psalms 3–7. Psalms 6 and 7 tell of His night of tears and of His loud cries to God before He goes to Jerusalem into the winepress, the *gittith* (this postscript, which appears before the title of Psalm 8, should appear at the end of Psalm 7).

The poetic prophecies in the Psalms are characterized by a compression of ideas and an economy of expression. In them are many sudden changes of subject matter as exemplified in the following psalms. After the Lord speaks to God about His many foes that are rising up against Him, in Psalm 3:1–6, He looks forward to the day when He arises as King. He then will strike His foes on the jaw and break their teeth (Ps. 3:7–8).

The same sudden change of thought occurs in Psalm 7. After the Lord's loud cry against His pursuers, in verses 1–2, and His loud cry against Judas, in verses 3–5, He again looks forward to the day when He arises against His raging enemies. In that day, He will bring to an end the violence of the wicked (Ps. 7:6–9).

Poetry also does not provide the information that ties the Psalms together. To know why Psalm 7 is followed by Psalm 8, it is necessary to read John 12:1–11. John makes it known that six days before the Passover, Jesus was in Bethany where a dinner was given in His honor. Lazarus, whom He recently raised from the dead, sat at the table and Mary anointed the Lord with an expensive perfume. She intended it for His burial. The next day He began to fulfill Psalm 8, as He rode a donkey to Jerusalem.

As the Lord rode toward Jerusalem, the city came into view. He wept over it and said, If you, even you, had only known on this day what would bring you peace but now it is hidden from your eyes. The day will come upon you when your enemies will build an embankment against you and encircle you and hem you in on every side. They will dash you to the ground, you and the children within your walls. They will not leave one stone upon another, because you did not recognize the time of Gods coming to you (Luke 19:41–44).

God had made known the year and the day the Lord was to die. He said, Know and understand this, from the issuing of the decree to restore and rebuild Jerusalem, until the Anointed One, there will be seven sevens, and sixty-two sevens, (or 483 years) and the Anointed One will be cut off (Dan. 9:23–26a). Ignorance of what He said does not excuse them.

Psalm 8 covers the Lord's last five days until He sees the moon. The Passover full moon indicates that He now will be made a little lower than the angels. Afterward, God will crown Him with glory and honor.

What took place between Psalms 8 and 10 is detailed in John 12:17–17:26. Psalm 9, which is joined with Psalm 10 by an acrostic, is an account of the destruction of the nations, which will take place on a future Passover night. This is a supplement to Psalm 2.

Psalm 10:2–11 is a description of Judas, who is coming with a detachment of soldiers and officials to arrest Jesus. Psalm 11 tells of the Lord's arrest and Psalm 12 describes the falling away of His disciples. Then He is taken to the courtyard of the high priest where His enemy, in Psalm 13, triumphs over Him. In Psalm 14, all in the courtyard condemn Him to death because the high priest, according to verse 1, denied His testimony that He was the Son of God (Matt. 26:65).

Because the deeds done to Jesus by the high priest and the chief priests were corrupt, Psalm 15 lists the Lord's requirements of the priests who will live on the holy hill about His temple and serve Him during the kingdom age.

From Psalm 14, where the fool rejected the Lord's testimony and all in his courtyard considered Him worthy of death, He was taken directly to the cross in Psalm 16. The Psalms do not record His maltreatment before Pilate and his soldiers, for the psalms of Book 1 speak only of the opposition to Him by His people; it is they who plotted to kill Him and it is they who considered Him worthy of death.

In this series, beginning with Psalm 16, we hear His words, His requests, and His hearts desire until His death in Psalm 22.

In these psalms, the Lord repeatedly speaks of His presence with the Father, until the day the saints are with Him in heaven (Ps. 16:10–11; 17:15; 19:4c–6 and 22:22–26). But He speaks more about His great joy, when God gives Him victory over His enemies at the time He comes as King. He speaks of His rejoicing, when God bestows upon Him great glory, splendor, and majesty with eternal blessings (Ps. 18:32–50; 29:1–9; 21:1–13; 22:27–31).

The Lord's example, of looking ahead when He suffered, to the glories that await Him when He returns to the earth, should encourage the saints to do the same. For a persecution is coming, when the saints will be hated by all nations because of the Lord's name. Some saints will be flogged, some brought to trial, and some will be put to death. Many will turn away from the faith because they have no root (Matt. 24:9–13; Matt. 13:20–23). Here is a trustworthy saying: If we died with Him, we will also live with Him. If we endure, we will also reign with Him (2 Tim. 2:11–12b). Keep reminding them of these things are Paul's words to Timothy (2 Tim. 2:14).

Psalms 23–29 are a prophetic account of what took place during the three days the Lord's body was in the grave. After His death in Psalm 22, He and the thief, who asked to be remembered when the Lord comes into His kingdom, went to Paradise (Luke 23:42–43). This is a spacious place in the third heaven, where the tree of life is (Ps. 18:19; 2 Cor. 12:1–4; Rev. 2:7). When God raised Him up on the third day, all in Gods temple cried, Glory! (Ps. 29:9). And after His ascension in Psalm 29:10–11, He sings His song of thanks to God for bringing Him up from the grave (Ps. 30).

Throughout the church age to the present time, the Lord's people have been persecuted. Many, as they faced death, used the words of Psalm 31:5 for their final prayer: Into Your hands I commit my spirit; redeem me, O Lord. The following was also their hope: How great is Your goodness which You have stored up for those who fear You, which You bestow in the sight of men on those who take refuge in You. In the shelter of Your presence, You hide them from the intrigues of men; in Your dwelling, You keep them safe from accusing tongues (Ps. 31:19–20).

Psalm 32 presents the preaching of repentance for the forgiveness of sins in the Lord's name to all nations. All the nations under the leadership of a king, who will call himself the Christ, will hate and persecute the saints during the first half of the last seven years (Ps. 33:10–22). In Psalms 34–35, we hear them cry out to the Lord in their troubles. This worldwide persecution of the saints, the greatest ever, will suddenly terminate when they are resurrected in Psalm 36. But few are they who understand the numerous events, which are to take place or have their beginning at the appointed time of the end. God sealed this until the appointed time of the end, and only the wise understand what He has sealed (Dan. 12:4, 9–10).

In Psalm 37, the resurrected saints are to wait a little while until the wicked are no more, then they will inherit the land (Ps. 37:10–11). Psalms 38 and 39 describe God wrath, when He rebukes and disciplines men for their sins, during the Great Tribulation. And Psalms 40–41, which conclude Book 1, are the first two of the 75 that speak of the Lord's kingdom.

An outline for Book 1 appears at the end of this chapter. It is a one page view of this continued story, which begins with a plot to take the Lord's life and ends with the Lord as the God of Israel from everlasting to everlasting. There are reasons why this orderly prophetic account, concerning the Lord's suffering and resurrection, has not been understood or outlined. The first reason is that the commentators do not search out what God concealed from the Jews in the first verse of Psalm 1.

The second reason is due to a lack of understanding the purpose for the historic titles, of which there are thirteen. They are Psalms 3, 7, 18, 30 and 34 in Book 1; Psalms 51, 52, 54, 56, 57, 60, and 63 in Book 2; and Psalm 142 in Book 5. The title to Psalm 3 is, A Psalm of David. When He fled from his son Absalom. Just as David fled Jerusalem because of his son, so also the Lord flees Jerusalem because of Israel, His firstborn son (Ex. 4:22). These historic titles do not appear in their historic order. The events referred to in the titles of Psalm 7 and 34 took place before the event in the title of Psalm 3.

The same is true of the titles in Book 2. The title to Psalm 51 is A Psalm of David, when the prophet Nathan came to him after David had committed adultery with Bathsheba. The events in the titles of Psalms 52, 54, 56 and 57 took place before the event referred to in the title of Psalm 51. God is a God of order (1 Cor. 14:33). Therefore, the historic titles are to provide information for their prophetic order.

Furthermore, Psalm 51 appears in the Great Tribulation series, Psalms 49–59. During the forty-two months of the Great Tribulation, 144,000 Jews will be sealed as well as many Gentiles, a great multitude that no one could count from every nation, tribe, people, and language. Among those sealed there will be many who sinned like David. They will wash their robes white in the blood of the Lamb (Rev. 7:1–17).

Psalm 49 is a riddle and the key to it is in verses 12 and 20. The commentators who do not search out this riddle, do not know that a man, a king, becomes a beast at the beginning of the Great Tribulation, when he breaks his covenant and invades Jerusalem. At that time, Satan is cast down to the earth and he gives to this king his power, his throne, and great authority, which he exercises for forty-two months. He is given power to make war on the saints and to conquer them (Rev. 12:7–9; 13:1–7). When the saints whom he beheaded are resurrected, they become priests of God and serve the Lord during His 1000-year reign on earth (Rev. 20:4–6).

A third reason why the prophetic psalms are not understood is that the present day commentators apply what they read to some historic event in the day the psalm was written. They do today what has been done for many years in the past. This misapplied emphasis is voiced by William De Burgh, D.D., in his two volumes entitled *A Commentary on the Psalms*, published in Dublin in 1860. He begins his lengthy dissertation by quoting a previous writer who said, Of all the books in the Old Testament, said the learned Bishop Horsley, the book of the Psalms is the most universally read, but, I fear, as little as any understood. De Burgh follows this assertion by saying, This opinion will be found to be no less true now than it was then (Vol. 1, p.1).

The learned bishop assigns the principal cause for this lack of understanding to the misapplied labors of modern expositors, who have applied much ingenuity and learning to find the immediate subject of every Psalm, either in the history of the Jewish nation, or in the occurrences of the life of David (Vol. 1, p. 1). What the expositors did in 1860, as well as prior to that day, continues to be done today.

According to William De Burgh, the real cause for the lack of understanding the Psalms is The Prophetical character of this Book. He maintains that The Psalms can only be understood in proportion as our views of the Prophetic scheme are just and Scriptural (Vol. 1, p. 3). Many today hold views concerning the prophetic scheme that are neither just nor scriptural. They take out of context the unknown day and hour passages of Matthew 24 and 25 that speak of the Lord coming as king immediately after the Great Tribulation, and declare that they apply to the Lord's coming for the church at an unknown day and hour before the last seven years of this age begin. They do not know that when the sun and moon are darkened, immediately after the Great Tribulation, that they stand still in the heavens (Hab. 3:11). Time is kept by their movement. Therefore, no one but God knows how long they will stand still. Will it be for one day, two days or three days? Only God knows the day and the hour when His Son is to return to the earth as King (Matt. 24:36).

Jesus said, My teaching is not my own. It comes from Him who sent me. He who speaks on his own does so to gain honor for himself (John 7:16,18). He who teaches that the Lord will come for the Church at an unknown day and hour, speaks on his own and presumptuously. His prayer should be, Who can understand his errors? Cleanse me from secret faults. Keep back Your servant also from presumptuous sins; let them not have dominion over me. Then I shall be blameless and innocent of great transgression. Let the words of my mouth and the meditation of my heart be acceptable in Your sight, O LORD, my strength and my redeemer (Ps. 19:12–14 NKJV).

It is a great transgression to declare another time for the resurrection than that which God has set. This began to be done before George Walter Whitcomb wrote his song that begins with the words Jesus may come today. In 1938, the Rodeheaver Company renewed their copyright for this song. Since that year, more than 23,000 days have passed, and the Lord has not come. God has said, "If what a prophet proclaims in the name of the LORD does not take place or come true, that is a message the LORD has not spoken. That prophet has spoken presumptuously. Do not be afraid of him" (Deut. 18:22).

The imminent return doctrine, that Jesus may come any day, does not agree with the Scriptures that speak of the resurrection. The Jews observed the Trumpets Feast annually on the first day of their seventh month. They never knew what would take place on this appointed day (Lev. 23:23–25). It was a mystery. After the church age had come, Paul said, "Listen, I tell you a mystery: We will not all sleep, but we will all be changed in a flash, in the twinkling of the eye, at the last trumpet. For the trumpet will sound, the dead will be raised imperishable, and we will be changed" (1 Cor. 15:50–52).

Paul also gave the time for the resurrection, when he spoke concerning the coming of our Lord Jesus Christ and of our gathering to Him. He said, "Don't let anyone deceive you in any way, for that day will not come until the rebellion occurs and the man of lawlessness is revealed, the man doomed to destruction. He will exalt himself over everything that is called God or is worshiped, so that he sets himself up in Gods temple, proclaiming himself to be God" (2 Thess. 2:1–4). This he does when he breaks his seven-year covenant in the midst of those years and invades Jerusalem (Dan. 9:27; 11:31–39).

What Paul said above about the time of the resurrection is similar to what David said in Psalm 36:1–4 about the sinfulness of the wicked one who has no fear of God. He flatters himself in this regard with wicked and sinful words against God.

He does this at the time of the resurrection, which is presented in the remainder of Psalm 36.

It is troubling to know that those who proclaim that the Lord may come today do not prepare the listener for the persecution that is coming before they are resurrected. When that persecution comes and they are not resurrected, many of them will ask, When can I go and meet with God? They will say, My tears have been my food day and night. Being continually taunted by the foe, they will be downcast and disturbed (Ps. 42:1–11).

But he who knew this persecution was coming will say, I will extol the LORD at all times. . . . Glorify the LORD with me and let us exalt His name together. I sought the LORD and He answered me; He delivered me from all my fears (Ps. 34:1–4). Because of the many troubles, there will be many prayers and some saints will be brokenhearted and crushed in Spirit (Ps. 34–35). But troubles and fears suddenly cease when both high and low among men find refuge under the shadow of the Lord's wings. There they feast on the abundance of His house and He gives them drink from His river of delights (Ps. 36:5–9).

This persecution, prior to the resurrection, is presented seven times in the Scriptures. These seven Scriptures are given in outline form at the end of this chapter. Each successive Scripture gives additional information about this persecution. In the three gospel portions, the Lord warns and instructs the persecuted one how to conduct himself during this time. Because this time is now near, the reader is urged to peruse these portions and be prepared to endure what is coming. Jesus gave similar words and additional instructions in Matthew 10:17–31. His instructions are followed by these words: Whoever acknowledges Me before men, I will also acknowledge him before My Father in heaven. But he who disowns Me before men, I will disown him before My Father in heaven (Matt. 10:32).

Outlines appear in our modern study Bibles for each book except the Psalms. In the introduction of the NIV Large Print Study Bible there is a section entitled, *Introductions to Books of the Bible*. The third paragraph begins with this line: A complete outline of the books content is provided in each introduction (except for the introduction to Psalms) (p. xiv. 10th Anniversary Edition, © 1995 by Zondervan Corporation).

Our present day Bible scholars have been unable to present an outline for the Psalms because they do not understand how the story in them begins. They are seemingly unaware that the first two psalms, which serve as an introduction to the entire Psalm collection, each speak of a plot against the Lord to take His life. They do not begin with this plot, because they do not search out what God, in His secret wisdom, kept hidden from the Jewish rulers in Psalm 1:1 (1 Cor. 2:8). Instead of beginning with this plot, they begin with the blessed man, who is typical of the multitudes that do not walk, stand, or sit in agreement with the wicked council that took counsel against the Lord. The delight of this blessed multitude is in the Lord's Word, upon which they meditate day and night.

Because these Bible Scholars do not search out what God concealed, they do not see the connection between Psalm 1:1 and Psalm 3, where the Lord flees Jerusalem because of the plot to take His life. They do not understand that the Holy Spirit spoke prophetically through David after he had fled Jerusalem because of his son Absalom.

The Psalms, as stated previously, present an orderly account concerning the Lord, one that begins with His last days as a prophet and ends with the glory of His reign as King. The order of the events concerning Him in the Psalms is the same as the order of the Lord's appointed feasts as presented in Leviticus 23. These appointed feasts are based on the Jewish calendar where the first day of every month begins when the new moon appears at twilight. Thus, when the moon is full at twilight, it is the fourteenth day of the month.

The following is the order of the Lord's appointed days in Leviticus 23: On the fourteenth day of the first month is the *Passover* Feast. At twilight, in the evening of that day, Israel is to kill the lamb that typifies the Lamb of God. Three days later they observed the *Feast of First Fruits*, which is symbolic of the Lord's resurrection. Fifty days later they were to observe the *Feast of Weeks*, which represented the coming of the Holy Spirit. And one verse, Leviticus 23:22, metaphorically describes the church age. The three feasts, that precede the church age, have been fulfilled.

On the first day of the seventh month, Israel observed the *Trumpets Feast*. What was to take place on this day in the future was a mystery, until the apostle Paul made that mystery known (1 Cor. 15:51–52). He declared that the Lord Himself will come down from heaven, with a loud command, with the voice of the archangel and with the trumpet call of God, and the dead in Christ will arise first. They and those still alive will be caught up together to meet the Lord in the air. Thereafter, we will be with Him forever (1 Thess. 4:16–17).

The time for the next two feasts, as given in Leviticus 23, was a temporary arrangement, so the people of Israel could observe all of them in a given year. But the *Day of Atonement*, the day the Lord returns to the earth as King, takes place immediately after the great tribulation, or three and one half years after the resurrection of the saints. On this day, the Lord will send His angels with a loud trumpet call, and they will gather His elect from the four winds, from one end of the heavens to the other (Matt. 24:29–31).

The Israelite who attends the seven-day *Feast of Tabernacles*, is to bring the first fruits of his labors and of the abundance of his harvest. On the first day, with choice fruits and leafy branches in hand, they are to rejoice before the Lord. On the last day, the great day of the feast, they pour out water before the Lord, to signify the pouring out of His blessings and Spirit in the Kingdom age (John 7:2, 10, 37–39; Isa. 44:3–5).

In Leviticus, the Lord's appointed feasts or days are presented in one chapter, but numerous chapters are use to speak of them in the Psalms.

Passover. Psalms 10–22 speak of this day. In Psalms 16–22, while the Lord is on the cross, we hear His words, His prayers and His hearts desire. After His death in Psalm 22:21, He speaks of the many who will praise Him for His suffering for them. In the presence of the congregation of His brothers in heaven, He will declare the name of His Father. The poor will eat and be satisfied; those who fear the Lord will praise Him. Eventually, all the ends of the earth will turn to Him and bow down before Him. They will feast and worship, kneeling before him. Posterity will serve Him; future generations will be told about the Lord. They will proclaim His righteousness to a people yet unborn (Ps. 22: 22–31).

Firstfruits. On the third day following His death, God raises Him from the dead and He becomes the first fruits of those who have fallen asleep (Ps. 29:1–9; 1 Cor. 15:20). His ascension is presented in Psalm 29:10–11 and in Psalm 30, He sings His song of thanks to God for bringing Him up from the grave.

Feast of Weeks. There is no special psalm for Pentecost. The Holy Spirit comes throughout the church age to him who confesses his transgressions to the Lord and is forgiven the guilt of his sin. The Holy Spirit comes to be his instructor, counselor, and guide (Ps. 32:1–8). The Spirit is Gods seal. He who is sealed is in Christ; he belongs to God. The seal is a guarantee of his inheritance until the time of his redemption (Eph. 1:13–14).

Feast of Trumpets. What is to happen on the first day of the seventh month was a mystery until Paul made it known that our resurrection would occur at the sounding of the last trumpet. And a mighty angel swore that the mystery would be accomplished when the seventh angel sounds his trumpet (1 Cor. 15:5–52; Rev. 10:5–7). When the seventh angel sounded His trumpet, loud voices in heaven said, The kingdom of the world has become the kingdom of our Lord and of His Christ, and He will reign forever and ever. . . . The time has come for judging the dead, and for rewarding Your servants the prophets and Your saints and those who reverence Your name, both small and great and for destroying the destroyers of the earth (Rev. 11:15–18).

The resurrection of the saints is presented in Psalms 36–37 of Book 1 and in Psalms 45–48 of Book 2. According to Daniel 12:1–3, this resurrection takes place at the appointed time of the end, which is the time when Satan is cast out of heaven and the Great Tribulation begins. Therefore, Psalms 37–38 and Psalms 49–59, which describe the Great Tribulation, immediately follow the resurrection psalms.

Day of Atonement. This day, which comes immediately after the forty-two months or the 1260 days of the Great Tribulation, is the great day of God Almighty. It is a day of battle and war, when the darkened sun and moon stand still in the heavens. It is also a Passover night, when the Lord comes and the Israelite is to be awake (Matt. 24:29–30; Hab. 3:11; Rev. 16:14–15). Some of the many events taking place on this day are detailed in Psalms 2 and 9 of Book 1, Psalms 60–64 of Book 2, Psalms 75–83 of Book 3 and Psalms 90–91 of Book 4. During the darkness of this long night, when the Lord is trampling His and Israel's foes, every Israelite who calls upon the Lord will be saved and protected (Ps. 91:9–16). In the morning of this day, the Lord comes from heaven with His glorified saints to Zion where He is installed as King (Ps. 68:1–35; 78:65–72; 110:1–7).

Feast of Tabernacles. This joyful feast, which originally was for seven days in the seventh month, will be extended in the kingdom age from one new moon (the first day of a month) to the next and from one Sabbath to another. During these days, all mankind will come to Jerusalem year after year, to worship the King, the Lord Almighty, and to celebrate the Feast of Tabernacles (Isa. 66:23; Zech. 14:16). Many will come from the east and the west and will take their places at the feast with Abraham, Isaac, and Jacob and all the prophets of God (Matt. 8:11; Luke 13:28–29).

Scattered among the seventy-five psalms that speak of the kingdom age, there are twelve psalms that definitely speak of the peoples of the nations coming with gifts and assembling in His courts to worship the King, to sing His praises and to kneel before Him. These are Psalms 66–68 and 72 of Book 2, Psalms 86–87, and 89 of Book 3 and Psalms 96, 98, 99,100 and 102 of Book 4.

All men come to Him, who is the hope of the ends of the earth, who stilled the roaring of the seas and the turmoil of the nations. They fear Your wonders (Ps. 65:1–8). All the earth shouts for joy;

they sing the glories of His name and say, How awesome are Your deeds! So great is Your power that Your enemies cringe before You. All the earth bows down before Him, they sing praises to His name (Ps. 66:1–4). The nations sing for joy because He rules them justly. All the ends of the earth fear Him (Ps. 67:3–6).

You are awesome, O God, in Your sanctuary; the God of Israel gives power and strength to His people (Ps. 68:35). All kings will bow down to Him and all nations will serve Him. All nations will be blessed through Him, and they will call Him blessed (Ps. 72:11,17). The name of the LORD will be declared in Zion and His praise in Jerusalem when the peoples and the kingdoms assemble to worship the LORD (Ps. 102: 21–22).

Because the people who assemble before the Lord are of many languages, that all of them may call on the name of the Lord and serve Him shoulder to shoulder, the Lord will purify the lips of the peoples (Zeph. 3:9). In that day, five cities in Egypt will speak the language of Canaan and swear allegiance to the LORD Almighty. . . . The Egyptians and Assyrians will worship together. . . . And Israel will be the third, along with Egypt and Assyria, a blessing on the earth (Isa. 19:18; 23–24).

According to the above, God is not the author of confusion, for He has given an orderly account of the Lord's appointed feasts and appointed the day when they are to be fulfilled. This ends the account of them in the first four Books of the Psalms.

The Genesis Psalms

Introduction - Two plots against the Lord			
Psalm	01	The Sanhedrin plots to take his life	*Ps. 1:1; Jn. 11:47-53*
	02	Kings and nations plot against the Lord and Israel	
His Suffering in Ephraim			
Psalm	03	The Lord flees from his foes to the town of Ephraim	*John 11:54*
	04	In distress, he calls for relief and sleeps	
	05	In the morning, he sighs and cries; he requests and waits	
	06	In agony and anguish, his tears flood his bed	
	07	His loud cries against his enemies and Judas	
His Suffering in Jerusalem			
Psalm	08	He rides a donkey into Jerusalem (His last five days)	
	09*	Passover night - He destroys the wicked nations	
	10*	Judas (described in vv. 2-11) comes with a crowd to arrest Jesus	
	11	God observes the righteous and the wicked	
	12	His faithful flee; they lied	
	13	God hides his face from the Lord until - see text	
	14	Fool, the High Priest, said, "There (he) is no God"	
	15	The priests who shall dwell on the Lord's holy hill in the Kingdom	
	16	Passover day - David foresaw and spoke of his death	*cf. Acts 2:25-31*
	17	His prayer for vindication	
	18	His song to God who avenges him with victory over all his foes	
	19	The heavens and the Law decree his death	
	20	His heart's desire	
	21	His heart's desire is granted	
	22	He dies - His name is proclaimed and men turn to him	

**Acrostics: 9 - 10*

The Genesis Psalms
Continued

Resurrection		
Psalm	23	He walks through the valley of the shadow of death
	24	He will ascend God's holy hill
	25*	Voices from the grave who hope in the Lord
	26	Vindicate me. I love the house where your glory dwells
	27	He asks to dwell in God's house till his enemies fall
	28	His cry is heard. He will give thanks to God in song
	29	His resurrection. All in God's temple cry, "Glory!"
	30	His song to God who lifted him up and healed him
Preaching		
Psalm	31	He is the refuge and resurrection of all the saints
	32	Preaching repentance and forgiveness of sins
	33	The King, his wars, famines and death (same as seals 1-4 Rev. 6:1-8)
	34*	Persecution of the saints (34-37 = same as seal 5, Rev. 6:9-11)
	35	Persecution of the saints and their many prayers (same as seal 5)
	36	Resurrection. The high and low feast in God's presence
The Great Tribulation		
Psalm	37*	They shall inherit the land when the wicked are cut off
	38	A Memorial for the great tribulation saint (See NAS title)
	39	A weeping sojourner waits for the Lord
The Lord's Kingdom		
Psalm	40	He saw the many wonders the Lord did for him at his coming
	41	The Lord seats him in the presence forever. Praise the Lord! Amen and Amen

**Acrostics: 24, 34, 37*

The Fifth Seal

The Persecution and the Resurrection

Rev. 6:9-11

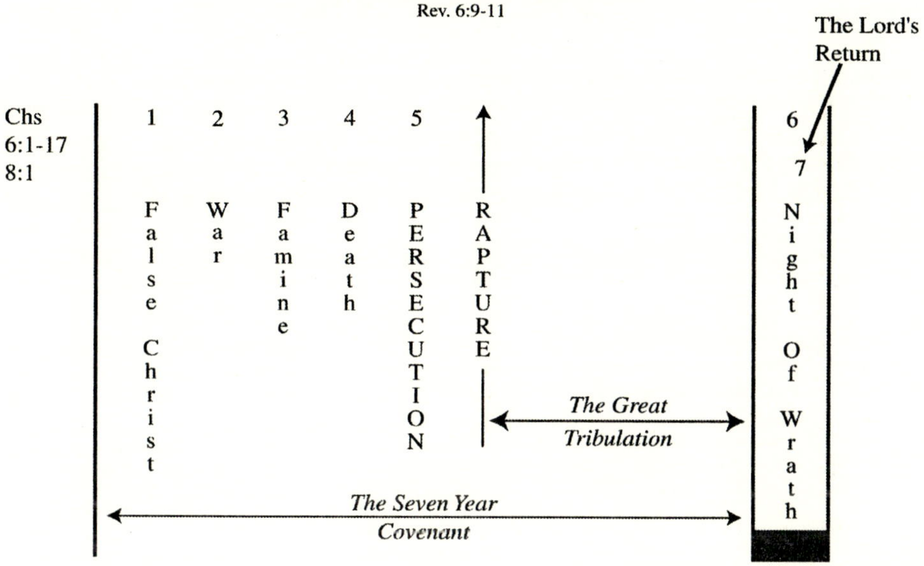

The First Six Accounts of the Persecution Before The Rapture

Psalms 33-35	**Psalms 42-44**	**Daniel 11:21-35**	**Matthew 24:5-13**	**Mark 13:6-13**	**Luke 21:8-19**
The King 33:16		A Vile Person 21	False Christ 5	False Christ 6	False Christ 8
War 33:16		War 22-31	War 6	War 7	War 9
Famine 19			Famine 7	Famine 8	Famine 11
Death 19	Death 11, 22	Death 22-26	Death 9	Death 12	Death 16
Persecution Chs. 34-35	Persecution Chs. 42-44	Persecution 33-35	Persecution 9-13	Persecution 9-13	Persecution 12-19
Rapture Ch. 36	Rapture Ch. 45	Rapture 12:2	Be Saved 13	Be Saved 13	Be Saved 19

Chapter 2

A Sealed Book

The Psalms, as a sealed book, are a manifestation of Gods secret wisdom, a wisdom that has been hidden and that God destined for our glory before time began (1 Cor. 2:7). Solomon, to whom God gave a wise and understanding heart, said, It is the glory of God to conceal a matter; to search out a matter is the glory of kings (Prov. 25:2). It was for His glory that God concealed the matter concerning His Son in the first 30 psalms until He fulfilled what was written. God then blessed us with every spiritual blessing in Christ, for He chose us in Christ before the creation of the world and adopted us as His sons through Jesus Christ, to the praise of His glorious grace (Eph. 1:1–6).

God concealed the prophecy concerning His Son in the first verse of the first psalm, which was written by David about a 1000 years before the Lord appeared on earth to fulfill what was written. For Christ was a mystery, a mystery hidden for long ages past. God kept this hidden in the days of the Lord's public ministry, for the people, who heard and followed Him, did not know that He was the Christ. He then asked the twelve, Who do you say I am? Peter answered, You are the Christ, the Son of the living God. Jesus warned them not to tell anyone that He was the Christ (Matt. 16:13–20).

None of the rulers of the Jews who comprised that wicked council referred to in Psalm 1:1, understood Gods secret wisdom, a wisdom that had been hidden before time began, for if they had, they would not have crucified the Lord of glory (1 Cor. 2:6–8).

No one among the Jews understood that Jesus was to die in Jerusalem and be raised on the third day. Even though the Lord explained this to the twelve three times, they did not understand any of this. Its meaning was hidden from them, and they did not know what He was talking about (Matt. 16:21–32; 17:22–23; 20:17–19; Luke 18:31–34).

Because the concealed matter in Psalm 1:1 and its connection with Psalms 3–7 is not searched out by the commentators today, this book about the Lord cannot be understood. About 50 years after the Lord fulfilled what was written about Him in the Psalms, John makes it known in his gospel that it was the Sanhedrin, the supreme council and tribunal of the Jews, with the high priest at its head, that plotted to take the Lord's life (John 11:45–57).

Because of this plot, the Lord could no longer walk openly among the Jews. He, with His disciples, fled Jerusalem to the region near the desert, to a village called Ephraim, where He stayed a few days. His words and prayers, His night of tears and loud cries to God, during His brief stay, are foretold by the Spirit through David in Psalms 3–7.

No one understood that these psalms applied to Christ, until He had fulfilled what was written about His night of tears in Psalm 6, and about His loud cries to God in Psalm 7. After He had fulfilled what was written in these psalms, the writer of Hebrews said, During the days of Jesus life on earth, He offered up prayers and petitions with loud cries and tears to the One who could save Him from death, and He was heard because of His reverent submission. Although He was a Son, He learned obedience from what He suffered and, once made perfect, He became the source of eternal salvation for all who obey Him and was designated by God to be High Priest in the order of Melchizedek (Heb. 5:7–10).

Without the words of the apostle in John 12:1–11, no one would know what took place between Psalm 7 and Psalm 8, between His stay in Ephraim and His riding a donkey into Jerusalem. As Jesus rides into Jerusalem on a donkey, to fulfill the prophecy of Zechariah 9:9, those going before Him and those following after shouted His praises as King by saying what is written in the first and last verses of Psalm 8. Only after Jesus was glorified did they realize that these things were written about Him and that they had done these things to Him (John 12:16).

Psalm 8, which covers the Lord's last five days, ends with Him seeing the moon. The Passover full moon announced to Him that His day to die had come. After He is made a little lower than the heavenly beings, God will crown Him with glory and honor. Much took place between Psalms 8 and Psalm 10, where Judas and others come to arrest Him. Abbreviated accounts of this time are given in Matthew 26:17–46, in Mark 14:12–42 and in Luke 22:7–45. But a detailed account of this time is given in John 12:17 to 18:3.

Psalm 9, which foretells the destruction of the nations, is united with Psalm 10 by an acrostic. Just as the Lord's times of trouble began when He was about to be arrested in this immediate Passover night, even so the troubles of the nations in Psalm 9 will begin in a future Passover night when they are destroyed (Ps. 10:1).

The Lord's times of trouble began in Psalm 10 when Judas with others came to arrest Him. Psalm 10:2–11 is a good description of the Lord's betrayer. Beginning with verse 12, the Lord looks forward to the day He arises as King, for Judas will then be called to account and his arm (power) will be broken. Thereafter, this man of the earth, (who is to come up out of the earth (Rev. 13:11–17), will terrify no more. His judgment is described in Psalm 109:6–20, where verse 8 is quoted by Peter in Acts 1: 20 and applied to Judas.

In Psalm 11, Jesus and His disciples see Judas and those with Him approaching in the shadows of their torches and lanterns and they see their arrows set against the bowstrings to shoot at the upright in heart. His disciples suggest that He flee. God in heaven is observing both the righteous and the wicked; He hates those who love violence. The Lord loves justice and the upright in heart will see His face.

When Jesus is arrested in Psalm 12, His disciples do what they said they would not. They fall away; they lied. The Lord is taken to the courtyard of the high priest where the wicked did freely strut about as they sought false witnesses to testify against Him (Ps. 12:8; Matt. 26:57–60).

The Lord asks in Psalm 13, How long will My enemy triumph over Me? Who is His enemy in the court of the high priest? It is the rulers of Israel and their followers, from whom God hid the knowledge that the One they are about to condemn is the Christ.

Fool, the high priest in Psalm 14, denies the Lord's testimony that He is the Christ the Son of God. Then all in the courtyard condemned Jesus to death, and the deeds they did to Him are vile. No one does Him good, not even one. He sees a day coming, during the Great Tribulation, when evildoers will devour His people like bread. Then He says, Oh, that salvation for Israel would come out of Zion! When the Lord restores the fortunes of His people, let Jacob rejoice and Israel be glad!

Psalms 14 and 53 are the same, except that Psalm 53 is entitled A Maskil (for instruction). Psalm 53 is in the series, 49–59, that describe the Great Tribulation. These saints need to be instructed concerning Fool, the beast. But not so in Psalm 14. The Lord knows all men. Just as Fool and all in his courtyard condemn Jesus as worthy of death, even so Fool, the beast, and his followers will behead the great tribulation saints (Rev. 20:4–5).

The priests in Psalm 15, who are to dwell about the Lord's Temple in Zion, will not be like those in Psalm 14. The Lord will require of them a blameless walk and that they do righteousness. They will despise the vile man and honor those who fear the Lord. The rules regarding them in Ezekiel 44:5–31 will be observed.

The Lord, who is considered worthy of death in Psalm 14, is taken directly to the cross in Psalm 16. The Psalms do not speak of Him appearing before the Gentiles, where evil is done to Him by Pilate and his soldiers and by Herod and his soldiers. In the psalms of Book 1, it is the Jews who are His enemies. It is their rulers who plot to kill Him and they desire to fulfill it. What took place between Psalms 14 and 16 is recorded in the four gospels (Matt. 27:1–33; Mark 15:1–22; Luke 23:1–33; John 18:28–19:18).

From the cross, in Psalm 16, the Lord speaks of the saints in the land as the glorious ones in whom is all His delight; He also mentions His inheritance in Israel's land when He becomes King (Ezek. 45:1–8). Peter quotes Psalm 16:6–11 in Acts 2:25–28 as evidence that David foresaw and spoke of the resurrection of Christ. The Lord speaks to His Father, saying, You will not abandon Me to the grave, nor will Your Holy One see decay. You have made known to Me the path of life; You will fill Me with joy in Your presence, with eternal pleasures at Your right hand.

As for His foes in Psalm 17, He asks God to vindicate Him. And I—in righteousness I will see Your face; when I awake, I will be satisfied with seeing Your likeness.

Confronted with death, in Psalm 18, the Lord cries for help. God hears and shakes the earth in His anger. The heavens part and the cherubim fly. From the dark rain cloud around them, there come hailstones, bolts of lightning, and thunder to rout His enemy. God reaches down to bring His Son to a spacious pace, to Paradise (Luke 24:43). Here God keeps His lamp burning. The Lord looks forward to the day when God avenges Him and arms Him with strength to pursue and crush His enemies. When God subdues the nations under His feet, He will praise God among the nations for His great victories and His unfailing kindness.

The apostle Paul quotes from Psalm 19 these words, Their voice goes out into all the earth, their words to the ends of the world, as proof that the Jews heard the good news. But the gospel was not accepted by all of them (Rom. 10:16–21). The proclamation of Jesus Christ was a mystery hidden for long ages past (Rom. 16:25). Gods intent was that through the church His manifold wisdom should be made known (Eph. 3:10). As for the Jews, God gave them a spirit of stupor, eyes so they could not see and ears so they could not hear, to this very day (Rom. 11:8).

Psalms 20 and 21 speak of the desire of the Lord's heart. His desire is for victory over His enemies in the day of His coming as King. Then the Israelites will shout for joy and the Lord will rejoice with great joy when God places a crown of pure gold on His head and bestows upon Him splendor, majesty, and eternal blessings.

What Psalm 22 declares concerning the death of Christ, no Israelite understood, for God hid it from them. Among those about His cross who scorned, despised, and insulted Him were strong bulls from Bashan who, like roaring lions, opened their mouths wide against Him. As He dies, the Gentile dogs, who pierced His hands and His feet cast lots for His clothing. After death had come, He looks forward to the day when He stands in the presence of God with the great congregation of those who fear Him. Then, in their presence, He will declare that God did not despise or disdain what He suffered for them. God listened to His cry for help. They will eat in His presence, be satisfied and praise Him. And when He rules over the nations, all the ends of the earth will turn to Him and bow down before Him; they will feast in His presence and worship Him. Their posterity will tell future generations about the righteousness He provided and they in turn will tell those yet to be born what He has done.

What took place after the Lord's death, while His body is in the grave, is presented in Psalms 23–28. In Psalm 23, we hear the voice of one who will eventually dwell in Gods house forever. We hear the request of the King of Glory in Psalm 24. And three voices from the grave are heard in Psalm 25, which is an acrostic. *Alpha, Alpha,* begins 25:1–3, to indicate it is the Lord's voice and request. In verses 4–7, it is the request of a saint. The request of a great tribulation saint is presented in 15–21. These three represent the first resurrection (Rev. 20:4b–6). The great tribulation saint will be raised when the Lord redeems Israel (Ps. 25:22).

In Psalm 26, the Lord requests vindication and redemption with the promise that when His feet stand in the great assembly, I will praise the LORD. The Lord looks forward, in Psalm 27, to the day He destroys the army advancing against Him while He is in the shelter of Gods tabernacle. He will sing and make music to His Lord when His head is exalted above His enemies. He is confident that He will see the goodness of the Lord in the land of the living.

The Lord cries again for mercy regarding His resurrection in Psalm 28. Because He trusts in God He is helped. His heart leaps for joy and He promises to give Him thanks in song, which He will do in Psalm 30.

In Psalm 29, as God displays the power of His mighty voice at the resurrection of His Son, all His mighty angles ascribe to Him glory and strength and all in his temple cry Glory! This psalm closes with an account of the Lord's ascension, for, in Psalm 30, He sings to God His song of thanks for bringing Him up from the grave, as He promised to do in Psalm 28:7.

As stated previously, no Israelite understood that Jesus was to die and be resurrected on the third day, for it was hidden from them. They did not understand these prophetic psalms that spoke of these events, even though they read them. The same is true of Psalms 31–36 that speak of the church age, for the gospel was a mystery, which is Christ in you, the hope of glory. God kept this hidden for ages past. Not until the Holy Spirit had come did men proclaim the unfathomable riches of Christ, in whom are hidden all the treasures of wisdom and knowledge (Eph. 3:8; Col. 2:3).

A double blessing is given the man whose sins are forgiven. The Lord is his hiding place when trouble arises on earth. Until that day of trouble comes, he has the Holy Spirit, the eye of God, as his instructor and guide in the way. For this, he is to rejoice, to sing and to shout for joy (Ps. 32).

Psalm 33 through 37 cover the first half of the last seven years of this age and Psalms 38–39 describe the last half, which is the Great Tribulation. What is to take place in the middle of these last seven years, or at the appointed time of the end, is sealed (Dan. 12:4). The Lord spoke to the prophet, beginning with Daniel 11:29, about various events that are to take place at the appointed time of the end. The last of the events mentioned is an account of the resurrection. Immediately thereafter, He said to Daniel, Close up and seal the words of the scroll until the time of the end. Many will go here and there to increase their knowledge [about it] (Dan. 12:4). It is the wise who will instruct many before their resurrection at the appointed time of the end (Dan. 11:33–35).

Likewise, the Lord swore with uplifted hand, in the presence of Daniel and two angels, that the astonishing things He spoke about would be fulfilled in three and one half years. Daniel, who heard this but did not understand, said, My Lord, what will the outcome of all this be? The Lord replied, Go your way, Daniel, because the words are closed up and sealed until the time of the end. Many will be purified, made spotless and refined, but the wicked will continue to be wicked. None of the wicked will understand, but those who are wise will understand (Dan. 12:5–10).

God sealed the events that are take place in the middle of the seven years and the events that will take place during the last three and one half years. But the wise will understand this: When the power of the holy people has been finally broken, all these things will be completed (Dan. 12:7).

As stated above, Psalms 38 and 39 speak of the Great Tribulation, and in the morning of the day that immediately follows, the Lord will return as King. Psalms 40 and 41 are the first two of the seventy-five psalms that speak of His reign. In Psalm 41, it is the great tribulation saint that is raised up and seated in His presence.

An outline entitled *The Five Books Of The Psalms* appears at the end of this chapter. This outline, which includes Book 1, shows the chapters and the Books that cover the last seven years of this gentile age, which is immediately followed by the Day of Atonement and the kingdom age.

Because half of the Psalms speak of the Lord's kingdom, every Christian should be interested, for we will reign with Him. The Lord's inheritance is the people of Israel (Joel 3:2). Repeatedly, the promise is made that we will inherit the land of the nations. These promises, concerning our inheritance and the fulfillment of them, are presented in Psalms 37, 45, 47, 111 and 112.

God, in His great mercy, has given us a new birth into a living hope through the resurrection of Jesus Christ from the dead, and into an inheritance that can never perish kept in heaven for you (1

Pet. 1:3–4). God has appointed the day for our glorification, when we will appear in His presence, worship Him, and feast on the abundance of His house (Ps. 36:8). While there, the Lord will judge and reward His prophets and every saint, small and great (Rev. 11:18). He will also choose our inheritance, which we will receive when He subdues the nations under our feet (Ps. 47:3–4).

Immediately after the Great Tribulation and after the Lord has destroyed the nations during that prolonged night of the Day of Atonement, He will come from heaven in the morning of that day to be installed as King on Mount Zion. He rides the ancient skies above in His chariot, the cherubim (1 Chron. 28:18). And we, with rejoicing, will follow in our chariots 10,000 times 10,000 and thousands of thousand (Ps. 68:4,17). We will come dressed in fine linen, white and clean and each will be wearing the golden crown received on the day of our resurrection (Rev. 19:14; Ps. 45.9).

After the Lord is enthroned in Zion, we will be seated on thrones and will be given authority to judge (Rev. 20:4). For 1,000 years, each saint, arrayed in holy majesty, will rule over the inheritance the Lord has chosen for Him, according to what he has done.

The Five Books of the Psalms

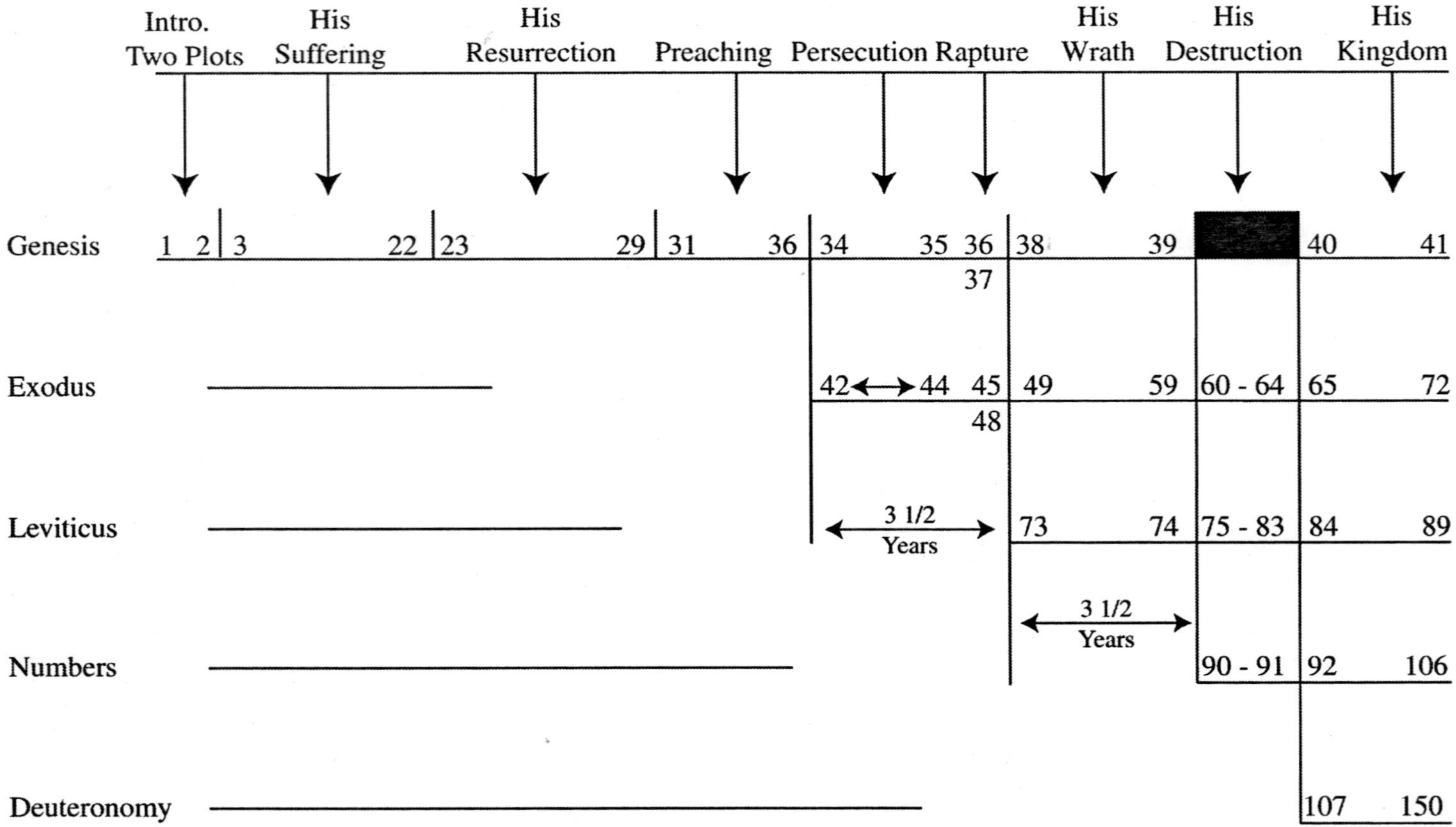

A Sealed Book

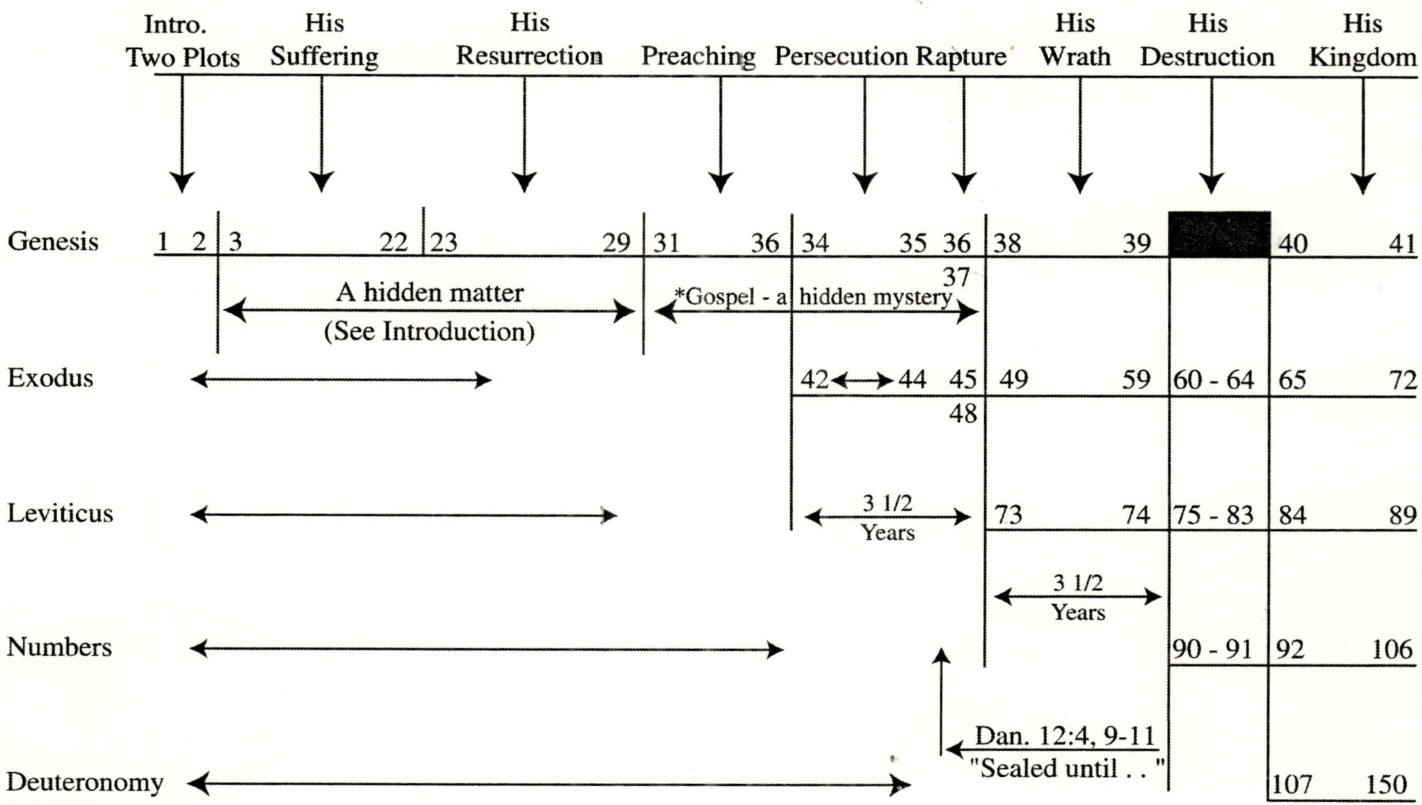

*Eph. 6:19; Col. 1:24-25

Chapter 3

A Complex Book

It was God who designed the Psalms to be the longest and the most complex book in the Scriptures. The assembling of the 150 diverse prophetic portions comprising this book was a complex procedure. It was the Holy Spirit that spoke through the authors who penned these varied prophecies during a span of approximately 900 years.

This span of time began when Psalm 90, *A Prayer of Moses*, was written about 1444 B.C. Moses wrote this prayer because the Lord, in His wrath, shortened the life span from 120 years to 70 or 80. He did this because Israel rebelled against His leadership at Kadesh in the wilderness of Paran, when He was about to lead them into the land He promised to give them. In this prayer, Moses entreats the Lord to relent, to turn from His wrath, that they might have joy all their days. The Lord will answer this prayer when He returns as king. He then will gather them into their land and satisfy them with long life and show them His salvation. He will destroy the shroud that covers all nations and will swallow up death forever (Ps. 92:12–15; Isa. 25:7–8).

This span of 900 years ends with Psalm 137, which was written sometime after Israel returned from their Babylonian captivity in 538 B.C. It was during this time span that the Spirit of God spoke prophetically through the men who authored the Psalms. These authors and the number of Psalms they penned are: David (73), Asaph (12), the sons of Korah (11), Solomon (2), and one each by Moses, Ethan and Heman.

These prophets spoke only what the Spirit gave they to say. They did not speak on their own authority. David testified to this in his oracle when he spoke his last words. He said, The Spirit of the LORD spoke through me; His word was on my tongue. The God of Israel spoke, the Rock of Israel said to me. He then wrote what the Spirit said to him. What the Spirit said about the Lord remains to be fulfilled (2 Sam. 23:1–7).

It was through the influence of the Holy Spirit that the 150 poetic prophecies were assembled and arranged in an order to tell a prophetic story about the Lord. This prophetic story begins with a plot to take His life: Psalms 3–30 speak of the Lord's death, resurrection, and ascension, which brought an end to His life at His first coming. And the last 59 psalms, 92–150, present the glories of His reign that follow His return as King.

Only the Holy Spirit could produce this prophetic masterpiece of poetic literature that can be likened to a musical drama that opens by introducing two plots against the Lord. The plot by the Jews to kill Him was fulfilled when He willingly laid down His life. The second plot, by the Gentiles, takes place immediately after the Great Tribulation, when the armies of the nations advance against the Lord to devour His flesh. Their plot will be in vain. The Lord will dash them to pieces like pottery (Ps. 27:2; 2:9). In the morning, after the night of battle, He will return as King and His reign will continue as long as the sun and moon endure.

Centuries passed following the assembling of this complex Book before the prophecies concerning the Lord's death and resurrection began to be fulfilled. Since that day, almost 2000 years have passed and, at present, all that follows Psalm 32 remains to be fulfilled. Therefore, only the Holy Spirit, who knows the thoughts of God and the end from the beginning, could assemble these psalms into a prophetic order that majors on the Lord's first and second comings.

The greatest complexity of the Psalms is the arrangement of them into five books. This five-book arrangement by the Spirit has mystified the best Bible students from centuries past to the present time. But the New Testament writers understood them. The writer of Hebrews quotes from the Old Testament thirty-two times; seventeen of the quotes are from the Psalms. And of the 283 New Testament quotations from the Old Testament, 116 of them are from the Psalms, according to *Haley's Bible Handbook*, Billy Graham Crusade Edition, p. 182.

Up to this present time, no one has understood or recognized the theme that unites the five books. The *MacArthur Study Bible* has two pages of comments before the Book of the Psalms. On page 742, these words appear under *Outline*: No one configuration key unlocks the mystery as to the organizing theme of this 5 Book arrangement. Thus, there is no identifiable thematic structure to the entire collection of the Psalms. It is also for this reason that there is not an outline provided for the Psalms in any of our modern study Bibles.

Concerning the thematic structure of this five-book arrangement of the Psalms, I was enabled by the Lord and my ever-present Teacher to see the thematic structure of the Psalms. These are the Lord's promises: My Father will give you whatever you ask in My name. You may ask Me for anything in My name, and I will do it. Concerning my Teacher, He said, The Holy Spirit, whom the Father will send in My name, will teach you all things (John 16:23,14:14, 26). I praise God for Him, who glorifies the Lord by taking what is His and making it known to me (John 16:14). I also glory in the promise that His presence with me is a guarantee of my inheritance, which the Lord will choose for me when He subdues the nations under the feet of the Church. We then will rule and judge the earth with Him in His kingdom (Eph. 1:18, 22: Ps. 47:1–4).

The outline showing the organized theme of this five-book arrangement is presented at the end of this chapter. It is entitled,

Events Similar To The Six Seals. The arrangement of the Psalms into five books is similar to the arrangement of the six seals in Revelation 6:1–17. The first five seals take place in the first half of the last seven years and the sixth seal, the destruction of the nations, takes place immediately after the Great Tribulation, or after the last seven years have come to their end.

The similarity to the first four seals of Revelation 6:1–8 appear in Psalm 33:10–19, where reference is made to the king, his wars, the famine, and death. These are similar to the first four seals. When seal one is opened, the rider on a white horse is given a crown and goes forth bent on conquest. When seal two is opened, the rider on a red horse is given a large sword and men slay one another. When seal three is opened, the rider on a black horse holds a scale in his hand and a voice says, "A quart of wheat for a days wages and three quarts of barley for a days wages." And when seal four is opened, the rider on a pale horse is named Death, and Hades was following close behind him. They were given power over a fourth of the earth to kill by sword, famine and plague, and by the wild beasts of the earth.

After the king, the war, the famine and death are mentioned, this statement is made by the saints in Psalm 33:20: We wait in hope for the LORD . . . in Him our hearts rejoice. Their resurrection is near; it will take place at the opening of the fifth seal when each is given a white robe.

When seal five is opened in Revelation 6:9–11, John sees the souls under the altar who were slain because of the Word of God and the testimony they maintained. With a loud voice they cry out, How long, Sovereign Lord, holy and true, until You judge the inhabitants of the earth and avenge our blood? They were each given a white robe and told to wait a little longer, until a number of their fellow servants and brothers were killed as they had been. The number of their fellow servants that are killed during the Great Tribulation is given in Revelation 7:1–17. They all are beheaded (Rev. 20:4–6).

The brief account of the persecution of the saints in seal five is enlarged upon in Psalms 34 and 35. And the similarity to giving a white robe to each of them is the resurrection of the saints in Psalm

36. Also, the instruction to wait a little longer, until God judges the inhabitants of the earth and avenges their blood, is similar to the instructions in Psalm 37, where they are told to wait patiently for a little while until the wicked are no more. Then the meek will inherit the land (Ps. 37:7, 10–11). Their wait for a little while will be during the Great Tribulation, which is presented in Psalms 38–39, 49–59 and in Psalms 73–74.

The similarity to the persecution of seal five is also presented in Psalms 42–44 of Book 2. And the similarity to receiving a white robe is the marriage of the King and His Bride in Psalm 45 and a likeness to their waiting a little while is in Psalms 46–48, as well as Psalms 49–59, which speaks of the great tribulation.

When seal six is opened, a great earthquake removes every mountain and island. The sun and moon are darkened and the skies recede. Then men, from kings to slaves, hide in caves and among the rocks of the mountains. They call to the mountains and the rocks, Fall on us and hide us from the face of Him who sits on the throne and from the Lamb! For the great day of their wrath has come, and who can stand? (Rev. 6:12–17).

Seal six in Revelation 6:12–17, which takes place immediately after the Great Tribulation, is the same as bowl seven of Gods wrath in Revelation 16:17–21. When this bowl is poured out, the cities of the nations fall because of the earthquake. It is the greatest ever to occur. And huge hailstones from the sky fall upon men. So terrible is this plague that men curse God because of it. This destruction of the wicked immediately after the Great Tribulation is told in Psalms 60–64 of Book 2, Psalms 75–83 of Book 3 and Psalms 90–91 of Book 4. After each account of the destruction of the nations, the psalms that follow speak of the Lord's reign as King.

This five-book arrangement of the Psalms makes it the most complex in the Scriptures. However, he who acquires an understanding of the arrangement of its content will declare it to be logically arranged. Its orderly arrangement makes it possible to repeatedly speak about the events that are to take place without becoming monotonous. And additional information is imparted concerning these events where they are retold.

EVENTS SIMILAR TO THE SEVEN SEALS

Pss.		
	BOOK 1	
33	The king of the nations, his army, famine and death. (33:10, 16-19)	Similar to seals 1-4 (Rev. 6:1-8)
34-35	Persecution of the saints. *(During first half of last 7 years)*	Similar to seal 5 (Rev. 6:9-11)
36	The resurrection of the saints. *(Middle of 7 years)*	
37	Wait a little while, and you will inherit the land.	
38-39	The great tribulation. *(Last half of 7 years)*	
40-41	The Lord comes; great tribulation saint is resurrected.	
	BOOK 2	
42-44	Persecution of the saints. *(During the first 4 seals)*	Similar to seal 5 (Rev. 6:9-11)
45-48	Resurrected saints in heaven during the great tribulation.	
49-59	The great tribulation.	
60-64	The destruction of the nations.	Similar to seal 6 and bowl 7*
65-72	The Lord is enthroned in Zion.	
	BOOK 3	
73-74	The great tribulation.	
75-83	The destruction of the nations.	Similar to seal 6 and bowl 7*
84-89	The Lord is enthroned in Zion.	
	BOOK 4	
90-91	The destruction of the nations.	Similar to seal 6 and bowl 7*
92-106	The Lord is enthroned in Zion.	
	BOOK 5	
107-150	The Lord is enthroned in Zion.	

**(Rev. 6:12-16; 16:17-21)*

Chapter 4

A Distorted Book

TITLES and POSTSCRIPTS

The Bible did not have chapter and verse numbers until the Geneva Bible, an English translation, was published in 1560. This small home edition, which became very popular, was the Bible the Pilgrims brought with them to America. The value of the chapter and verse numbers in the Bible is not all positive. It was not a work of the Holy Spirit, for he who placed the chapter numbers in the Psalms added to the difficulty of understanding this book, which already was the least understood book in the Scriptures.

Robert Estienne, a printer, added the verse numbers and the publishers of the King James Version, in 1611, followed the chapter divisions made by Archbishop Stephen Langdon in 1551. The work of both men is faulty. As for the Psalms, the archbishop did not recognize the difference between the postscript at the end of a psalm and the title of the next psalm that followed it. Ignorant of this fact, the archbishop placed the chapter numbers between the last verse of the psalm and its postscript. This caused all postscripts to appear before the titles of the following psalm, where their directives do not apply. They are there to this day.

This faulty work made it very difficult for a psalm reader to understand the titles because of the presence of a postscript before them. And what this did to the psalm reader, it also did to the commentators and expositors who produced our modern study Bibles. Because they accept the misplaced postscript as part of the title, they give obscure explanations to the difficult and misplaced words they do not understand. Evidences of this are the numerous footnotes that say, Possibly a literary or musical term. This confusion, caused by the bishops defective work, will never end until his mistakes are recognized and corrected. This could have been done when our modern study Bibles were published, because of what was already known.

This faulty work was exposed by James William Thirtle, LLD. D.D., in his book entitled, *The Titles Of The Psalms*, published by Morgan and Scott, LD., London, in 1916. It was he who took note that there was a psalm in Habakkuk 3:1–19 that was a model for those in the Book of the Psalms. Its title is, *A Prayer of Habakkuk according to Shigionoth* (New American Standard (NAS); Revised Standard Version (RSV)). Its postscript is, *For the choir director, on my stringed instruments*. Because this postscript ends the psalm, as well as the book, it could not be made to appear before the title of the next psalm.

Dr. Thirtle also points out the confusion before Psalm 88 because of the misplaced postscript of Psalm 87. Was Psalm 88 written by the Sons of Korah or by Heman the Ezrahite? When the long postscript is returned to Psalm 87, where it applies and agrees with that title, then what is left is the title to Psalm 88. It is *A Mask of Heman the Ezrahite*. As for the words in the postscript of Psalm 87, According to *mahalath leannoth* or singing with dancing, they describe how Psalm 87 should be sung. For they, who come from the nations to worship the Lord in Zion, sing and dance when they are born again and the Lord inscribes their names in His Book. By contrast, there is no joy in the context of Psalm 88.

For his second example of confusion, Dr. Thirtle points to the title of Psalm 56, where the words of the postscript of Psalm 55 appear. They are, According to Jonath elem rehokim (NAS) or According to the dove on Far-of Terebinths (rsv). When this postscript is returned to Psalm 55, it agrees with verses 6–8 that say, Oh, that I had the wings of a dove! I would fly away and be at rest. . . . I would hurry to my place of shelter, far from the tempest and storm. The above postscript is not a tune and neither are the words Shiggaion, Shigionoth, Miktam or Maskil.

What James William Thirtle made known through his book more than eighty-six years ago was discussed by many in the years that followed. What he disclosed was referred to in commentaries and reckoned with in Bible dictionaries and encyclopedias in English, German, French, and Italian. The Jews, the Protestants, and the Catholics knew about it. And many who had been in the seminary I attended in 1955 had read his book, for it was worn and needed to be rebound. Why then was this erroneous work by the archbishop not corrected in one of our modern study Bibles? This could and should have been done. Instead of correcting this faulty work, some modern translations contribute to the problem.

In *The New English Bible*, published in 1970, all the titles and postscripts were removed and only the title to the psalm in Habakkuk 3 remains. It remains because Robert Estienne erroneously designated it to be a verse. *The Living Bible* (Paraphrased) was published in 1971. Only 11 of the 117 psalm titles appear in it and only the postscript of Habakkuk 3 is recorded.

In 1996, the *Life Application Study Bible*, also called *The New Living Translation*, was published. In this Bible, the words of the misplaced postscripts were mixed with the words of the titles. And the difficult words, such as *Shiggaion, Miktam* and *Maskil* in the titles and *Gittith* in the postscripts were eliminated. Progressively, with the coming of new translations, the distinction between a psalm title and a postscript has been obliterated, and the understanding of their contribution to the context is almost, if not altogether, impossible to obtain. The titles and the postscripts are just as much a part of a psalm as are the words between them. The Holy Spirit, who knows the thoughts of God, influenced the psalm writers to assign the proper words to each title and postscript so the purpose of God for each psalm might be understood.

A listing of all titles and the meaning of their difficult words appear below. The same is true of the postscripts. The chapter numbers presented apply to the psalm where the postscript should appear. Following this listing, comments concerning the titles and the postscripts are given to show how appropriate they are to the context where they are found.

TITLES

Historical Titles 3,7,18,30,34, 51,52,54,56,57,60,142

A Shiggaion of David (A loud cry) 7

A Miktam (Involves death) 16,56,57,58,59,60

A Prayer 17,86,90,102,142

Of David the servant of the Lord 18,36

A Song 30,45,46,48,65,66, 67,68,75,76,83,87,92,108,120–134

A Maskil (For instruction) 32,42,43,44,45,52,53,54,55, 74,78,88,89,142

A Petition (To bring to remembrance NKJV; *For the memorial offering RSV) 38,70

A Song of Love 45

A Psalm. A Song for the Sabbath Day 92

A Psalm. For giving thanks 100

A Psalm of Praise 145

POSTSCRIPTS

For the director of music

On stringed instruments (Neginoth) 3,53,54,,66,76

For flutes 4

With stringed instruments. According to Sheminith (Eight stringed lyre) 5,11

According to Gittith (Wine press) 7,80,83

According to Muth-labben (Death to the Son) 8

According to the Doe of the Dawn 21

For Jeduthun (The praising one) 38,61,76

According to Lilies (Shoshannim) 44,68

According to Alamoth (Alma = young women; women's voices) 45

According to Mahalath (Mahal = dancing) 52

According to the Dove on Far-off Terebinths (Oaks) 55

According to Do Not Destroy (Al-tashcheth) 56,57,58,74

According to Lilies of the Covenant (Shoshannim-Eduth) 59,79

According to Mahalath Leannoth (Dancing with singing) 87

THE TITLES

Historical Titles. These titles appear throughout the prophetic story. Psalms 3 and 7 are the first and last that tell of the Lord's sufferings after he fled Jerusalem to the city of Ephraim near the desert. Originally, the prophetic words of Psalm 18 were spoken by David in 2 Samuel 22:1–51, but were the words spoken by the Lord from His cross. Psalm 30 was the Lord's song of thanks to His Father, after His ascension, for raising Him up from the grave. Psalm 34 is the first to speak of the persecution of the saints prior to their resurrection and Psalms 51, 52, 54, 56 and 57 describe the Great Tribulation. Psalms 60 and 63 declare the destruction of the nations and 142 is a cry of one wanting relief from his troubles, that he may return to Israel's land.

A Shiggaion. The Lord's loud cries in Psalm 7 are verified in Hebrews 5:7.

A Miktam. Peter quotes Psalm 16:8–11 in Acts 2:25–28 to speak of the Lord's death. The Miktams of Psalms 56–59 proclaim death to the great tribulation saints and Psalm 60 declares the destruction of the nations, when the Lord tramples His enemies.

A Prayer. Psalm 17 is the Lord's prayer from the cross. In Psalm 86, the nations that come to worship the Lord in Zion request to be taught His way that they may fear Him with an undivided heart. Psalm 90 is Moses request for the restoration of the life span. The request in Psalm 102 by those serving the Lord in Zion is for their children to live in the Lord's presence as well as their descendants. In Psalm 142, a troubled Israelite requests mercy that he may dwell in Israel.

Of David, the Servant of the Lord. God delivers His servant from His enemies forever in Psalm 18. He arms Him with strength for the battle against His foes and makes Him head of the nations. In Psalm 36, the Lord delivers His servants from their enemies forever by taking them into His refuge until the wicked have fallen.

A Song. The Lord sings Psalm 30 to God after His ascension. The saints sing Psalms 45–46 and 48 after they are resurrected. The Israelites sing Psalms 65–67 and 68 after the Lord returns to Zion. The righteous in heaven sing Psalms 75–76, and 83 after the Lord brings down the horns of the wicked and lifts up the horns of the righteous. In Psalm 87, those coming from the nations to worship the Lord in Zion sing and dance when they are born there and the Lord records their names. In Psalm 92, all who enter the Lord's Sabbath rest will make music and sing; they will proclaim the Lord's love from morning to night, even to old age. In Psalm 108, the Jew will begin to sing while still among the nations, in the morning of the Lord's return. After He teaches them His Law, they will sing the Songs of the Ascents, Psalms 120–134, when they ascend the fifteen steps into His courts.

A Maskil. In Psalm 32, the blessed man, whose sins are forgiven, receives the Holy Spirit as his instructor. In Psalms 42, 43, and 44, instruction is given to the persecuted saints and the resurrected Bride is given instruction in Psalm 45. The great tribulation saints are instructed, in Psalms 52–55, concerning the mighty man of lawlessness and his destructive followers. Psalm 74 informs how the enemy of God burned the sanctuary and every place of worship in the land. Psalm 78 proclaims how the Lord beats back His enemy and establishes His sanctuary on the heights of Mount Zion. Psalms 88 and 89 tell how the Jews call upon the

Lord, in their day of trouble, and proclaims His faithfulness and love throughout all generations. In Psalm 142, a former prisoner instructs the righteous gathered about him how he called upon the name of the Lord to set him free, that he might praise His name.

A Petition. Psalms 38 and 70 present the following petitions of the great tribulation saint: Do not let them gloat, May those who seek my life be put to shame and confusion and Come quickly to help me, O Lord my Savior. Psalm 70 begins with the word Hasten, and ends with the words, do not delay.

A Song Of Love. The song of Psalm 45 expresses the Lord's love for His Bride. He is anointed with the oil of gladness as He rides forth for her. Out of ivory palaces, the music of strings make Him glad. He is enthralled with her beauty as she enters His palace and acknowledges Him as her Lord. He promises to make her name to be remembered in all generations; therefore the peoples shall praise her forever and ever.

A Song For The Sabbath Day. According to Psalm 92, throughout the Sabbath age, the righteous will proclaim the Lord's love in the morning and His faithfulness at night. In the courts of the Lord they will flourish, grow, and bear fruit to old age. They will exalt the Lord and proclaim Him as their Rock. There remains, then, a Sabbath rest for the people of God. . . . Let us, therefore, make every effort to enter that rest (Heb. 4:9,11).

A Psalm For Giving Thanks. Psalm 100 declares that all the earth will come to worship the Lord in Zion. With shouts of joy, they will enter His courts to give thanks to His name for His goodness and enduring love throughout all generations.

A Psalm Of Praise. The Israelites, according to Psalm 145, will praise the Lord's majesty and might from generation to generation, that men may know His mighty acts and the glorious splendor of His everlasting kingdom. The final words of this psalm, Let every creature praise His holy name for ever and ever, serve as an introduction to the last five psalms that begin and end with Praise the Lord.

THE POSTSCRIPTS

For Flutes. These are used only in Psalm 4. In the forepart of this psalm the Lord is in distress; His suffering is intense. In verses 6–8, the Lord's heart will be filled with greater joy than when their grain and wine increase. The flute can express these diverse feelings. My heart shall wail like a flute for Moab (Jer. 48:36). And, when Solomon was anointed as King, All the people went up after him, playing flutes and rejoicing greatly (1 Kings 1:40).

According To The Gittith or winepress. As told in Psalm 7, Jesus knew that when He leaves the village of Ephraim near the desert for Jerusalem, His pursuers there, like a lion, would tear Him to pieces and His blood would flow as from a winepress. So also, in Psalm 80, Israel's blood will flow before He rescues and saves them. Likewise, the blood of the nations will flow as from a gittith, in Psalm 83, when the Lord destroys them.

According To Muth-labben. This postscript, The Death Of The Son, appears at the end of Psalm 8, after Jesus sees the Passover full moon. It announces that His day to die has come and God is about to make Him a little lower than the heavenly beings.

According To The Doe Of The Dawn. This postscript that follows Psalm 21 describes what the Lord will do after God grants Him His hearts desire. He desires victory over His enemies, to receive a crown of gold and to have length of days. He also desires great glory, splendor, majesty, and eternal blessings. Then, like a doe of the morning, He will ascend Mount Zion, where He will be exalted for His strength and might.

For Jeduthun. Jeduthun was one of the three chief musicians under David's direction. David, in the postscripts of Psalms 38 and 61, requests that Jeduthun lead the trained musicians and skilled singers when these psalms are presented before the Lord. Asaph did the same for Psalm 76. These psalms speak of Gods wrath. Psalm 38 speaks of His wrath during the Great Tribulation and Psalm 61 declares His wrath when He destroys the nations. Psalm 76 states that His wrath against men brings Him praise. The survivors among the nations who fear Him, make vows to Him and bring Him gifts. It requires a skilled leader of the singers to portray what is in the context of these three psalms.

According To Lilies. The lilies in Psalm 44 are the persecuted saints who have been brought down to the dust. In Psalm 68, they are the rejoicing saints, coming from heaven with Him who rides the clouds. Their chariots number 10,000 times 10,000 and thousands of thousands. They proclaim His majesty and power in His Temple to be awesome.

According To Alamoth. These maidens in Psalm 45 are the Lord's royal bride, the honored women in the ivory palaces and the virgin companions who enter into the Lord's palace on the day of His marriage.

According To Mahalath. In Psalm 52, the mighty man of evil boasts all day long during the Great Tribulation of his destruction and deceit. He grew strong by destroying others, but the Lord uproots him from the land of the living. This will be seen from the house of God by those he destroyed. They will laugh at him and *dance*; they will praise the Lord forever.

According To The Dove On Far-off Terebinths. Psalm 55 speaks of one who did not flee with Israel into the wilderness when the Great Tribulation began. Now, he is in trouble. He suffers as the wicked stare and revile him in their anger. The terrors of death and horror overwhelm him. With fear and trembling, he says, Oh, that I had the wings of a dove! I would fly away and be at rest, I would flee far away and stay in the desert; I would hurry to my place of shelter, far from the tempest and storm (Ps. 55:6–8).

According To Do Not Destroy. Psalms 56–58 and 74 describe how the enemies of Israel, during the Great Tribulation, are in hot pursuit of them to take away their life. The postscript to these Psalms is Do Not destroy. The Lord speaks about not destroying them all, when He said, As when juice is still found in a cluster of grapes and men say, Don't destroy it, there is yet some good in it, so will I do in behalf of my servants; I will not destroy them all. I will bring forth descendants of Jacob, and from Judah those who will possess My mountains; there will My servants live (Isa. 65:8–9).

According To Lilies Of The Covenant. This postscript to Psalms 59 and 79 describes the lilies the Lord will gather out of the Great Tribulation. They will be resurrected when the Lord returns as King and fulfills the covenant He made with Abraham concerning the land (Gen. 15:18).

According To Mahalath Leannoth. Those coming from the nations to Zion to be taught by the Lord will dance and sing after they are born in Zion and the Lord registers their names in His book.

THE ACROSTICS

The second distortion of this book took place when seven of the eight acrostics were removed from the Psalms as well as those in other books. This evidently was done about the time the chapter and verse numbers were added to the Scriptures. The deleting of the acrostics removed the messages implied by the presence of the acrostic as well as the messages presented at their irregularities. These messages are in addition to what is presented in the text.

God has repeatedly forbidden the adding to His Word and the taking away from it (Deut. 4:2, 12:32; Prov. 30:6; Rev. 22:18–19). God warns the transgressor that He will take away from him his share in the tree of life and in the Holy City. By removing the acrostics, what God declared by their presence has been taken away. The same is true of their irregularities.

There are four imperfect acrostics in Book 1 and they appear at Psalms 9–10, 25, 34 and 37. In Book 5, the perfect acrostics are the following: Psalms 111, 112, 119 and 145. The acrostics removed elsewhere should appear at Proverbs 31:10–31, Lamentations 1:1–22, 2:1–22, 3:1–66, 4:1–22 and Nahum 1:1–8, which is half an acrostic.

The acrostic in Proverbs 31:10–31 describes a wife of topmost value to her husband. Jeremiah's loud cries over the Lord's judgment of Jerusalem are unequaled and the Lord's topmost wrath is displayed when He takes vengeance on His enemies, according to Nahum.

Today, there is not an acrostic to be found in the following English versions: *The Revised Standard Version* (1952), *The New English Bible* (1970), *The Living Bible* (1971) and *The Life Application Study Bible* (1988). Only one acrostic, that of Psalm 119, appears in *The Septuagint Bible* (1954), *The New International Version* (1973) and *The New King James Version* (1985). The only modern version that records them all is a Catholic translation, *The Jerusalem Bible* (1966). If the *Jerusalem Bible* included them in 1966, most of the English translations above could have done the same.

David, under the direction of the Holy Spirit, appears to have pioneered the use of the acrostic as a tool to dispense additional information to that in the text of a psalm. He is the author of the four imperfect acrostics and the first, which unites Psalms 9 and 10, is the most complex. The perplexity over these imperfections has been given as the leading cause for the removal of them from the Scriptures, for these imperfections were extremely puzzling to the commentators and expositors. But ignorance of the Spirits purpose for them is not sufficient cause to delete them from the Word of God.

When the purpose for an acrostic and its irregularities are understood, they will be acclaimed as masterpieces of biblical literature, and Psalms 9 and 10 will top the list. A presentation of this acrostic with comments concerning the irregularities will verify this fact.

The title to Psalm 9 is *A Psalm of David* and the postscript, following Psalm 10, is *To the Chief Musician.* This indicated that these two psalms are designed to be a unit by the acrostic. The number to the left of the Hebrew letter indicates the verse. The first Hebrew letter to the right is the order of that letter in the alphabet and the second is the numeric value of that letter. And what is implied by the presence of these numbers is in accord with The Numeric Principle, pp. 100–123 in the book entitled *Principles Of Biblical Hermeneutics* by J. Edwin Hartell, Zondervan Publishing House, Grand Rapids, Michigan, 49506. (Let the reader understand that the Hebrew alphabet was used for numbers. The first ten letters had values from 1–10. Each successive letter increased in value by 10, and after the 19th letter, with it value of 100, each successive letter increased in value by 100, Thus the 22 letters ranged in value from 1–400)

Psalm 9		**Psalm 10**				**The 6 missing letters that refer to Judas**	
01 *Aleph* 1	1	01 *Lamedh*		12	30		
03 *Beth* 2	2					*Mem*	40
05 *Gimel* 3	3					*Nun*	50
06 *He* 5	5					*Samek*	60
07 *Vav* 6	6					*Ayin*	70
11 *Zayin* 7	7					*Pe*	80
13 *Heth* 8	8					*Tsadeh*	90
15 *Teth* 9	9	12	*Qoph*	19	100		
17 *Yodh* 10	10	14	*Resh*	20	200		
19 *Qoph* 19	100	15	*Shin*	21	300		
		17	*Tav*	22	400		

Topmost in these two psalms is times of trouble for the nations, in a future Passover night, when the Lord destroys the wicked; and times of trouble for the Lord and for Judas, in this immediate Passover night (Ps. 9:9; 10:1). In chapter 9, this acrostic has 10 Hebrew letters to indicate these nations are the ten-horned beast of Daniel 7:7. The fourth Hebrew letter, which is absent at Psalm 9:6, is replaced by the fifth letter. When this fourth beast is destroyed, then the saints of the Most High will receive the Kingdom (Dan. 7:17–18; 26–27). The destruction of these nations will be a fulfillment of Psalm 2.

The completeness of the destruction of the nations is amplified by the letter *Qoph,* with its numeric value of 100, which replaces the tenth letter. Ten is a complete number, but *Qoph* is 10 times 10. The Lord will not only destroy the nations that assemble against Him, but He will also destroy their descendants and uproot the cities from which these nations come. The destruction of them will be complete (Ps. 21:10; 9:6; Isa. 17:1–2).

The destruction of these nations will take place in a future Passover night as implied in the following passages. This Passover night will also be the Day of Atonement.

> *In the night when a holy feast is kept (Isa. 30:29, RSV).*

> *At the full moon on our feast day (Ps. 81:3, RSV).*

> *When the whole moon turned blood red (Rev. 6:12–17).*

> *At evening time before the morning, they are no more (Isa. 17:14).*

> *Lo, I am coming like a thief! Blessed is he who is awake (Rev. 16:12–17).*

Judas is described in Psalm 10:2–11 of this acrostic, for it is he who is coming with a large armed force sent by the chief priests and elders to arrest Jesus. The six missing letters from these verses that describe him indicate that he will be missing. Before this day is over, he takes his life. The total value of the six missing letters is 390 or 13 times 3 times 10. The number 13 is used with the word rebellion in Genesis 14:4. But three and ten are complete numbers. This indicates that his rebellion against the Lord was complete. When he arises, as the second beast in Revelation 13:11–17, his end on earth will again be on a Passover day. With the wicked, he will be removed from the earth. Then he and the first beast will be thrown into the lake of burning sulfur (Rev. 19:19–20).

The acrostic of Psalm 25 is in the series, chapters 23–29, where we hear the topmost voices of those who speak to God while their body is in the grave. In this acrostic, God gives ear to His Son, to the saints of the church age and to those saved during the Great Tribulation. The first voice is that of the Lord's uplifted soul.

1	*Aleph*	1	1	To you, O Lord, I lift up my soul;
2	*Aleph*			in you I trust, O Lord my God.

	Beth	2	2	Do not let me be put to shame, nor let my enemies triumph over me.
3	*Gimel*	3	3	No one whose hope is in you will ever be put to shame, but they will be put to shame who are treacherous without excuse.

The double *Alpha* declares that it is the Lord who cries out to God. Using the Greek language, the Lord said, I am the *Alpha* and the *Omega* (Rev. 1:8). Note the promise of the Lord in verse 3 above, for one such is speaking in verses 4–7.

4	*Daleth*	4	4	Show me your ways, O Lord, teach me your paths;
5	*He*	5	5	guide me in your truth and teach me, for you are God my Savior, and my hope is in you all day long.
6				Remember, O Lord, your great mercy and love, for they are from of old.
7	*Zayin*	7	7	Remember not the sins of my youth nor my rebellious ways;

The missing sixth Hebrew letter, the number for man, who was created on the sixth day, signifies that this man was killed. He, like the Lord, must also wait for his appointed day to be resurrected. Regarding the third voice from the grave, this great tribulation saint must also wait for his day to be resurrected. His requests are given in verses 16–22 of this Psalm.

This portion speaks of a great tribulation saint. All of them will be beheaded. This portion ends with the letter *Pe*, which has a value of 80. By eliminating the 0, we have the basic 8. The Lord was raised from the dead on the first day of the week, which was the eighth day. His name, Jesus, in the Greek, has a value of 888 (The Greek alphabet was also used for numbers) This great tribulation saint missed the resurrection day for the church. He therefore must wait for his resurrection until the day the Lord redeems Israel (verse 22).

This time of trouble takes place during the rule of the fourth beast (Dan. 7:7). This is indicated by the double *Resh* in verses 18–19. The double of 200 is 400. By removing the zeros, we have the basic 4, representing the rule of the fourth beast who will devour the whole earth, trampling it down and crushing it (Dan. 7:23).

Psalm 34, the third irregular acrostic, speaks of the topmost persecution of the Church during the first half of the last seven years, which are the days of the false christ, of wars, of famines, and earthquakes (Matt. 24:5–8). The first three verses of Psalm 34 present a standard of conduct for the saint during these days. The next four verses bear evidence that this saint did not fear those who kill the body but cannot kill the soul (Matt. 10:28).

The absence of *Waw*, the sixth letter of the Hebrew acrostic, indicates that this saint has been killed. This fulfills what Jesus said, Then you will be handed over . . . to be put to death (Matt. 24:9). The final four verses of this psalm speak of the resurrection of the righteous man. The presence of *Pe* at the end has a value of 80. The basic 8 is the number for the resurrection. The Lord was resurrected on the first day of the week or on the eighth day; 80 is also the value of the word *new*. This righteous man will receive a new body when he is redeemed.

19 *Resh*	20	200	A righteous man may have many troubles; but the Lord delivers him from them all.
20 *Shin*	21	300	he protects all his bones; not one of them is broken.

21	*Tav*	22	400	Evil will slay the wicked; the foes of the righteous will be condemned.
22	*Pe*	17	80	The Lord redeems his servants; no one who takes refuge in him will be condemned.

Psalm 37 speaks seven times about the topmost inheritance the saints will receive when the wicked are cut off. An irregularity occurs where *Ayin,* the sixteenth letter, is united with *Lamedh,* the twelfth letter.

27	Samek	15	60	Turn from evil and do good, then you will dwell in the land forever.
28				For the Lord loves the just, and will not forsake his faithful ones;
	Ayin	16	70	They will be protected forever;
	Lamedh	12	30	but the offspring of the wicked will be cut off;
29				the righteous will inherit the land, and dwell in it forever.

The combined value of *Ayin* and *Lamedh* is 100. Ten is a complete number and 10 times 10 shows how complete the eternal protection of the saints will be and how complete the destruction of the wicked will be when their offspring are also cut off. So also the lands of the wicked inherited by the righteous will be complete forever.

In Psalm 110, the Lord has returned as the King of Israel and in the acrostic of Psalm 111, He is giving the lands of the other nations as an inheritance to His people. These people are the assembly of the upright. In the acrostic of Psalm 112, it is the saint who was gracious, compassionate, and righteous, who had scattered abroad his gifts to the poor, that will be blessed and remembered forever. His horn will be lifted high in honor. This will be seen by the wicked, who will gnash their teeth and waste away in their longing.

Psalm 119 is the longest chapter and the longest acrostic in the Scriptures. It is the Lord's topmost presentation of His Law to His people and to others that come to be taught by Him. Eight times an Israelite says, Teach me your statutes and seventeen times this promise is made: I will keep your statutes. Never before has this been the attitude of His rebellious and stiff-necked people. Isaiah foresaw and spoke of this day, saying, In the last days the mountain of the LORD's Temple will be established as chief among the mountains; it will be raised above the hills, and all nations will stream to it. Many peoples will come and say, "Come, let us go up to the mountain of the LORD, to the house of the God of Jacob. He will teach us His ways, so that we may walk in His paths." The Law will go out from Zion, the Word of the Lord from Jerusalem (Isa. 2:1–3).

Psalm 145, the last acrostic in this book, is a topmost exaltation of the Lord by those who witnessed His awesome works and mighty deeds when He destroyed the nations. As they celebrate His abundant goodness to them, they extol Him to each succeeding generation, that they might know the Lord's mighty acts and the glorious splendor of His everlasting kingdom.

Chapter 5

A Similar Book

The Jews called the five books of the Psalms The Little Books Of Moses for several centuries before Christ. Why they did this no one knows. If they saw a likeness between the first five books of the Bible and the five books of the Psalms, that similarity has never been published.

Modern Bible teachers have also called the five books of the Psalms The Little Pentateuch. In the early part of 1955, Dr. Charles W. Slemming, a noted Bible teacher and author from London, England, was holding his fifth series of Bible messages where I was the pastor. He had a 4 x 6 outline chart for every book of the Bible and, at each service, he displayed the chart for the book he was presenting. One day, he showed me his chart on the Psalms. Across its top were the names of the five books of the Law and below them, respectively, were his outlines for the five books of the Psalms. I asked, Why do you do this? He said, The Jews did this for several hundred years B.C. But he did not know why. In his presence, I vowed to find the similarity, but I was not aware of the high cost of gaining an understanding of what was unknown to men.

In the fall of 1955, I returned for my third year of seminary study to see if there was a writer who spoke about this similarity between the Psalms and the Pentateuch. I checked every book in that library on the Psalms. But the professor under whom I studied demanded that I write a twenty-two page paper on some subject concerning the Psalms to get credit for the course. After reading my paper on *How To Interpret The Psalms,* he said, I agree with your interpretation 100 percent, but that is not the way it is usually done. He refused to return my paper, saying. I want to write a book on the Psalms.

Later, I searched the books on the Psalms in the libraries of two other seminaries, a university, and two colleges. I visited stores that sold religious books and bought books from England. I finally concluded that it was necessary on my part to recognize the similarity in Genesis to that in the first book of the Psalms. This was accomplished with the aid of the Holy Spirit my teacher and counselor who was given to teach me all things (John 14:26).

The Genesis Similarity

The account in Genesis 22 of the willingness of Abraham to sacrifice his son as a burnt offering on a mountain in the region of Moriah prefigured the willingness of God to sacrifice His Son on that same mountain centuries later. Abraham was willing to do this because of the promise God had made the day Isaac was weaned and Ishmael was cast out or disinherited. God said, It is through Isaac that your offspring will be reckoned. Therefore, Abraham was willing to kill his son, for he believed God could raise Isaac from the dead to fulfill the promise He had made concerning him (Heb. 11:17–19).

There are similarities between Abraham's son and God's Son. The only words we hear from Isaac are his question. He said, Father, . . . the fire and wood are here . . . but where is the lamb for the burnt offering? Isaac trusted his father, who answered, God Himself will provide the lamb for the burnt offering, *my son* (Gen. 22:7–8, emphasis added).

Jesus knew He was the lamb to be sacrificed by God on that same mountain. When He was about to be arrested, He did not flee but willingly submitted to the plan of His Father. He did not answer His accusers, until the high priest demanded to know if He was the Christ, the Son of God. After His affirmative reply and testimony, Fool denied what He said and called it blasphemy. Then all those present in the courtyard of the high priest did Him no good thing. All their deeds were vile (Ps. 14:1; Matt. 26:62–68; Mark 14:60–65). The Lord fulfilled what Isaiah predicted: He was oppressed and afflicted, yet He did not open His mouth (Isa. 53:7).

Another similarity between these two accounts is what God said to Abraham after the symbolic death of his son and what is said after the Lord's death in Psalm 22. To Abraham, God said, I swear by Myself, declares the LORD, because you have done this and have not withheld your son, your only son, I will surely bless you and make your descendants as numerous as the stars of the sky and as the sand on the seashore. Your descendants will take possession of the cities of their enemies, and through your offspring all nations on earth will be blessed because you have obeyed Me (Gen. 22:14–18).

After the Lord's death in Psalm 22, He promised to declare Gods name to His brothers in that great assembly and they will eat and be satisfied and praise the Lord, who will say to them, May your hearts live forever! And when He rules over the nations, the ends of the earth will turn to Him and all nations will bow down before Him. Their posterity will serve Him and tell future generations about His righteousness, which He has provided (Ps. 22:22–31).

As a final similarity, Abraham received his son back from the dead, figuratively speaking, on the third day. God also raised His Son from the dead on the third day (Gen. 22:4; Heb. 11:19; Luke 24:1, 7, 46).

The Exodus Similarity

One similarity between Exodus and the second book of the Psalms appears in the opening chapters of each book. The Israelites were oppressed in Egypt because they had multiplied and spread in the land. Therefore the Egyptians put slave masters over them and oppressed them with forced labor, using them ruthlessly to build store cities (Ex. 1:11–14).

The Lord saw their misery and heard them cry out because of their suffering. He spoke to Moses and sent him to bring them out of Egypt to a land flowing with milk and honey.

In Psalms 42 and 43, the opening chapters of Book 2, we hear a weeping saint say, My soul thirsts for God, for the living God. And he asks, When can I go and meet with God? My tears have been my food day and night, while men say to me all day long, Where is your God? (By this, they imply that their christ is on the earth.) My soul is downcast within me. . . . My bones suffer mortal agony as my foes taunt me, saying to me all day long, Where is your God? . . . Why must I go about mourning, oppressed by the enemy? Send forth Your light and Your truth and let them guide me; let them bring me to Your holy mountain, to the place where You dwell.

In Psalm 44, it is the Jewish believers who are humbled and plundered by their adversaries. They are reproached and reviled by the taunts of their enemies, who are bent on revenge. For the Lord's sake, they face death all day long and are considered as sheep to be slaughtered. Awake, O Lord! Why do you sleep? Rouse Yourself! . . . Rise up and help us; redeem us because of Your unfailing love (Ps. 44:23, 26).

A second similarity is the coming of the Lord to lead the oppressed Israelites from Egypt to Mount Sinai. He will do the same for the oppressed saints at the close of the church age. He will come and lead them to Mount Zion.

The Lord came in a cloud on that Passover morning to lead Israel with a mighty hand from Egypt while the Egyptians were burying their firstborn. In the cloud, He went before them to guide them on their way. On the third month, they came to the foot of Mount Sinai and camped there for eleven months (Ex. 13:21).

The Lord's coming for the church and their stay in Mount Zion until they see Him subdue the nations under their feet is presented in Psalms 45–48. In Psalm 45, the Lord rides forth from heaven clothed with splendor and majesty. His sword is at His side. His sharp arrows pierce the hearts of His enemies and His right hand displays awesome deeds. The resurrected saints speak of His throne and kingdom. His royal bride is at His right hand and her sons will be made princes in all the earth

Psalm 46 describes a river that makes glad this city, the holy place where the Most High dwells. Here the Lord Almighty is with them until He brings desolation on the earth and makes wars cease to the ends of the earth. In Psalm 47, the Lord chooses the inheritance of each saint after he subdues the nations under their feet. For this they are to sing His praises.

According to Psalm 48, it was from Mount Zion, the city of the great King, that the saints saw the destruction of the forces of kings that advanced against the Lord. Those in Mount Zion rejoiced. They meditate in Gods temple on His unfailing love. Before leaving the city, they are instructed to walk about Zion, go around her, count her towers, consider well her ramparts, view her citadels, that you may tell of them to the next generation. For this God is our God forever; He will be our guide even to the end.

A third similarity is the encampment of the Israelites at the foot of Mount Sinai and the assembling of the saints in the city on Mount Zion. The Lord made it known to Moses that He would come down in a dense cloud on the third day, so the Israelites would hear the Lord speak to him and always put their trust in Moses. The Israelites were to wash their clothes and be ready for His coming, in the sight of all the people. Limits were put around the mountain for they were not to touch it, whether man or beast, for such would be killed. The mountain was set apart as holy (Ex. 19:9–15).

In the morning of the third day, there was a long blast of the rams horn calling all the people to come near the mountain. There was thunder, lightning, and a dense cloud over the mountain. A very loud trumpet blast caused all to tremble. As the Lord descended, smoke covered the mountain and billowed up like a furnace. The mountain trembled violently and the trumpet blasts became louder and louder. The Israelites heard the Lord speak to Moses. When He spoke to them His ten commandments, the people stayed at a distance and trembled in fear. They said to Moses, Speak to us yourself and we will listen. But do not have God speak to us or we will die. Moses said to them, God has come to test you, so that the fear of God will be with you to keep you from sinning. Although they heard God speak to Moses, they did not desire Him to speak to them. Neither did they cease to sin against the Lord (Ex. 19:16–19; 20:18–20).

These fearful Israelites were not to touch Mount Sinai and neither were they permitted to see the Lord who came down upon it. How different it is with the glorified saints on Mount Zion. In this city of God, the city of the Lord Almighty, they are with the Lord and He is with them. In Gods temple, they also meditate on Gods unfailing love for them. While in this city of God, they dwell in palaces adorned with ivory and are clothed in glorious embroidered garments interwoven with gold. They were made glad by the streams of the river in the city of God and had no fear when the Lord lifted His voice. When He caused mountains to quake and fall, causing earths waters to roar and foam. And, after He brought desolations on the earth, He lifted his voice and said, Be still and know that I am God; I will be exalted among the nations, I will be exalted in the earth. They had no fear for the Lord Almighty was with them. It was he who said, Come and see the works of the Lord Ps. 46:1–11).

The Leviticus Similarity

The Day of Atonement is the outstanding similarity between the book of Leviticus and the third book of the Psalms, 73–89. What the high priest annually did on the Day of Atonement, according to Leviticus 16, the Lord will do on this appointed day in the future, when He fulfills what is written in Psalms 75–83.

Prior to the Day of Atonement, wickedness increases like an infectious malady according to Leviticus 14 and 15. But, on the Day of Atonement, according to chapter 16, the Israelites are cleansed from all their sins. Thereafter, beginning with chapter 17, there is holiness in the land, because the Israelites obey the Lord's precepts and keep His commands.

Likewise in Psalms 73–74, prior to Day of Atonement, the arrogant wicked prosper. The peoples turn to them as they lay claim to heaven and take possession of Israel's land during the Great Tribulation. On the Day of Atonement, according to Psalms 75–83, the wicked are suddenly destroyed and Israel's sins are forgiven. Thereafter, as is told in Psalms 84–89, the forgiven Israelites yearn for the Lord's courts, where He bestows His favor upon them.

In Leviticus 16, the high priest takes the blood of the goat into the Most Holy Place and sprinkles it on and in front of the atonement cover. By this He makes atonement for the uncleanness and rebellion of the Israelites. According to Hebrews 9:11–14, this was typical of Christ taking His own blood into the Most Holy Place to obtain an eternal redemption. When the Lord does this on the Day of atonement, Israel's rejection of Him as the Son of God, their Savior, will end.

As the high priest comes into the Holy Place, the place of prayer and fellowship with the Lord, He sprinkles blood on the horns of the altar of prayer to cleanse it and to consecrate it from the uncleanness of the Israelites. After the Lord fulfills this on the Day of Atonement, Israel's prayers in that future night will be accepted. He will fellowship with them as their provider and protector in that night of destruction, even sending His angels to keep them from harm.

Coming outside to the brazen altar, the high priest sprinkles blood on the horns of the altar and on the altar seven times to cleanse it and consecrate it from the uncleanness of the Israelites. Then the Israelites, who have not accepted His sacrifice as their Savior to this very day, will request Him to be such to them on that Day of Atonement and He will save them and bring them back to their land.

When the high priest finishes making atonement for the Most Holy Place, the Holy Place and the altar, he lays both hands on the scapegoat (a type of the beast) and confesses over it all the wickedness and rebellion of the Israelites, and puts them on the head of the goat. He then sends it away to a solitary place in the wilderness, a place of no return. This beast, into whom Satan entered after He was cast down to the earth, is typical of the deceiver who leads the whole world astray. This solitary place for the beast will be in the lake of burning sulfur, a place of no return. Only he and the false prophet will be in it while Satan is bound with a chain in the abyss for 1,000 years (Rev. 12:9–13:3).

The two typical events that are fulfilled on the Day of Atonement are the cleansing of Israel and the sending away of the scapegoat. These two events, with supplementary information, are presented below in the nine psalms, 75–83. The scapegoat is the arrogant, boastful and wicked king who, with all those participating in the plot against the Lord and Israel, will be destroyed.

According to Psalm 75, the Lord chose the proper time to judge the earth and its inhabitants and to rebuke the arrogant, boastful and wicked king, who lifted up his horn on high. For in the Lord's hand is a cup of red wine fully mixed, which the wicked will drink to the dregs when He cuts off all the horns of the wicked.

In Psalm 76, the Lord's name is great in Israel where He, in His anger, broke the weapons of war. Valiant men are plundered, horse and chariot lie still and the land feared. It was quiet after God pronounced judgment and those who survived were restrained. Thereafter, men make vows and all the neighboring lands bring gifts to Him who is to be feared.

During the night of Gods great wrath, according to Psalm 77, lightning flashed, the skies resounded with thunder and the clouds poured down water. The earth trembled and quaked and a troubled Israelite cries out to God without ceasing. He groaned. His heart mused, as he though about Gods miracles, when He, with His mighty arm, redeemed His people from Egypt. But now He is redeeming them from the nations where He has scattered them.

Only what is said at the end of the long parable in Psalm 78:65–72 applies to this day of atonement. After the Lord had given over His people to the sword, He beats back His enemies and put them to a perpetual reproach. He then builds His sanctuary on Mount Zion and from there He shepherds His people.

The Lord, as foretold in Psalm 79, will pour out His wrath on the nations that invaded Israel and defiled His temple, that devoured Jacob and laid waste his dwelling place. He provides atonement for Israel's sins and avenges the blood of His servants. He returns to Israel's neighbors sevenfold the reproach they hurled at Him. After this, the Israelites are the sheep of His pasture and they will show forth His praise to all generations.

Repeatedly in Psalm 80, the Israelites ask the Lord to come and save them. They plead for His face to shine upon them. They vow to call upon His name and not turn back from Him. Three times they ask that He restore them. These requests will begin to be fulfilled when He returns in the morning of the Day of Atonement.

Psalm 81 speaks concerning the morning of this full moon day when the Israelites hear the sound of the rams horn. They sing for joy with shouts to God, their strength. They play the melodious harp and lyre and strike the tambourine, for the Lord removed their enemies, whose punishment will last forever. He will feed Israel on the finest wheat and satisfy them with honey from the rock.

In Psalm 82, the Lord arises to judge the assembled rulers for their walk in darkness, for their partiality toward the wicked and the injustice of their government. He calls them gods. But they are all sons of the Most High and will die like mere men. Then all the nations become His inheritance.

Psalm 83 is the fulfillment of Psalm 2. The Lord's enemies, who plotted to destroy Israel as a nation, are endeavoring to carry out their plot against the Lord. (They fully intend to topple Him from His lofty place. . . . They plan to shoot from ambush at the Innocent Man . . . suddenly, without fear. But God will suddenly shoot them with arrows; suddenly they will be struck down Ps. 62:4; 64:4, 7.) The Lord makes them like tumbleweed and chaff before the wind as He pursues them with His tempest and terrifies them with His storm. With dismay and shame they perish in disgrace. He lets them know that He is the Lord, that He alone is the Most High over all the earth.

The Numbers Similarity

A likeness of what is in Book 4 of the Psalms, 90–106, to what is in the book of Numbers has to do with the prayers of Moses. His prayer in Numbers 14, is not the same as his prayer in Psalm 90. Although both prayers speak of what took place at Kadesh, where Israel refused to enter the land because of the report of the spies, they deal with different matters.

Moses pleads for Israel in Numbers 14 when the Lord desired to destroy them with a plague because they treated Him with contempt and refused to believe in Him in spite of all the miraculous signs He performed among them. He desired to strike them down and make Moses become a greater and stronger nation than Israel.

The Lord gives ear to Moses plea with reasons why He should forgive them. This is His reply: I have forgiven them, as you asked. Nevertheless, as surely as I live and as surely as the glory of the LORD fills the whole earth, not one of the men who saw My glory and the marvelous signs I performed in Egypt and in the desert but who disobeyed Me and tested Me ten times—not one of them will ever see the land I promised on oath to their forefathers. No one who has treated me with contempt will ever see it. But, because My servant Caleb has a different spirit and follows Me wholeheartedly, I will bring him into the land he went to and his descendants will inherit it (Num. 14:20–24).

Then the Lord said to Moses and Aaron, How long will this wicked community grumble against Me? I have heard the complaints of these grumbling Israelites. So tell them, As surely as I live, declares the LORD, I will do to you the very things I heard you say: In this desert your bodies will fall every one of you twenty years old or more, who was counted in the census and who has grumbled against Me. Not one of you will enter the land I swore with uplifted hand to make your home, except Caleb son of Jephunneh and Joshua son of Nun. As for your children that you said would be taken plunder, I will bring them in to enjoy the land you have rejected. But you—your bodies will fall in this desert. Your children will be shepherds here for forty years, suffering for your unfaithfulness, until the last of your bodies lie in the desert. For 40 years—one year for each of the 40 days you explored the land—you will suffer for your sins and know what it is like to have Me against you. I, the LORD, have spoken, and I will surely do these things to this whole wicked community, which has banded together against Me. They will meet their end in this desert; here they will die (Num. 14:20–35).

According to Moses prayer in Psalm 90, he is troubled by what the Lord said after He forgave the wickedness of the Israelites. He is concerned about the life span which the Lord shortened from 120 years to 70 or 80. All who were numbered in the census were turned back to dust; they were consumed by Gods anger and terrified by His indignation; their days passed away under His wrath and ended with a groan. Their span of seventy or eighty years were but trouble and sorrow, and passed quickly in fear of His anger and wrath.

In his prayer, Moses said, Who knows the power of your anger? He therefore makes this request: Teach us to number our days aright, that we may gain a heart of wisdom. His next request in paraphrase is: O Lord, come back to us! How long will you delay? Then Moses said, Satisfy us in the morning with your unfailing love, that we may sing for joy and be glad all our days. Make us glad as for as many days as you have afflicted us, for as many years as we have seen trouble (vv. 14–15). He asks that the Lord's favor rest upon them.

Psalm 91 tells what the Lord will do for the Israelites in the night when He destroys His wicked enemies. He will save from the deadly pestilence every Israelite who trusts in Him. They will see

1000 fall at their side and 10,000 at their right hand, but no harm will come near their tent. For the Lord, their refuge, will command His angels to rescue and guard them. Those who love the Lord and call on His name in this time of trouble, He will answer, deliver, and honor. With long life He will satisfy them and show them His salvation.

Psalm 92 is entitled *A Song for the Sabbath Day*. Every Israelite who calls on the Lord during the night of the Day of Atonement will enter His Sabbath of rest. In the morning of that day, they will begin to sing and to proclaim His name. They will flourish in the courts of the Lord like a palm tree and will bear fruit to old age; they will always be fresh and green, for on Mount Zion, the Lord will destroy the shroud that enfolds all peoples. . . . He will swallow up death forever. The Sovereign Lord will wipe away the tears from all faces; He will remove the disgrace of His people from all the earth (Isa. 25:7–8).

The Deuteronomy Similarity

The similarity between Deuteronomy and Book 5 of the Psalms, 107–150, is the teaching of the Law by Moses to the Israelites before they enter the Promised Land and the Lord teaching the Law in Psalm 119 to the Israelites before they enter His temple courts.

Moses knew that Israel would not keep the Law he taught them, but He foresaw the day when they would return to the Lord and follow all His commands. He informs them that the Lord has not given them a mind to understand or eyes that see or ears that hear (Deut. 29:2–4).

The same was true when the Lord sent Isaiah to minister to them. He said, Go and tell this people: Be ever hearing, but never understanding; be ever seeing, but never perceiving. Make the heart of this people calloused; make their ears dull and close their eyes. Otherwise they might see with their eyes, hear with their ears, understand with their hearts, and turn and be healed (Isa. 6:9–10).

For this same reason Jesus spoke in parables to the crowds in His day. He kept from them the knowledge of the secrets of the kingdom of heaven, saying, Though seeing, they do not see; though hearing, they do not hear or understand (Matt. 13:10–13).

As Moses was about to conclude his teaching in the Plains of Moab, he said to them, Your children who follow you in later generations and foreigners who come from distant lands will see the calamities that have fallen on the land and the diseases with which the Lord has afflicted it. . . . All the nations will ask: Why has the LORD done this to this land? Why this fierce, burning anger? And the answer will be: it is because this people abandoned the covenant . . . He made with them when He brought them out of Egypt. They went off and worshiped other gods. . . . Therefore the LORD's anger burned against this land so that He brought on it all the curses written in this book. In furious anger and in great wrath the LORD uprooted them from their land and thrust them into another land, as it is now (Deut. 29:9–28).

It shall come to pass, when these blessings and curses come upon you, which Moses set before you, and you and your children return to the Lord your God and obey Him with all your heart and with all your soul, then the Lord your God will gather you again from the nations where He has scattered you. The Lord your God will circumcise your hearts and the hearts of your descendants, so that you may love Him with all your heart and all your soul, and live (Deut. 30:1–10).

Book 5 of the Psalms opens by speaking of those the Lord has redeemed from the hand of their foes and gathered in from the nations, from the east, the west, the north and the south (Ps. 107:1–3). Then one who has returned to the land will present this typical request: Open for me the gates of righteousness; I will enter and give thanks to the LORD. This is the gate of the LORD through which the righteous may enter. I will give You thanks, for You answered me; You have become my salvation (Ps 118:19–21). But before any of the righteous can enter into His courts, they must know and fully obey the precepts the Lord has laid down (Ps. 119:4). He will teach them His Word and way, as found in Psalm 119, and His blessed will walk according to His law; they will do no wrong. In this psalm, an Israelite repeatedly declares his love for the Lord's Word and vows to keep it with his whole heart forever and ever.

Those who have been taught the Lord's precepts will be privileged to ascend the seven steps through the gate into His outer court and the eight steps through the gate into His inner court (cf. Ezek. 40:22, 31). As they ascend each step, they sing in sequence one of the fifteen Songs of the Ascents, Psalms 120–134. And when in the Lord's presence, they sing The Great Hallel, Psalm 135 and 136.

Just as Book 4 closes with two Hallels, Psalms 105 and 106, so also Book 5 closes with five Hallels, Psalms 146–150. With these songs, which begin and end with Praise the Lord, Israel will praise Him for remembering His covenant and giving them the lands of the nations, and for doing for them that which He did for no other nation; He revealed His word to Jacob, His laws and decrees to Israel. Hallelujah!

In the last two psalms, 149 and 150, where the Israelites are assembled in His sanctuary, they sing a new song of praise to their King for His surpassing greatness and for crowning them with His salvation. Being so honored, they are joyful and dance as they play instruments of music with the praises of the Lord in their mouths. With their unending praises they present this request, Let everything that has breath praise the Lord. Hallelujah!

Chapter 6

A Hallelujah Book

Hallelujah is a shout of joy, praise, or gratitude and a common form of adoration and thanksgiving in Jewish worship. The root of the forepart of this compound word is *halal,* to praise, and the *jah* (Hebrew *yah*) is rendered Lord or Jehovah. The words *Praise the Lord* appear at the beginning and at the end of the last two psalms of Book 4 and the last five psalms of Book 5. These are Psalms 105, 106 and 146–150. Because of the misplaced chapter number for Psalm 105, the words Praise the Lord, which should begin Psalm 105, are found at the end of Psalm 104. The words, Praise the Lord (*Hallelujah*) stand alone four times in Book 4 and seventeen times in Book 5.

We will present the *Hallelujahs* as they appear in their prophetic order. The glorified saints, who came from heaven with their King, are the first to express their joy and gratitude to the King in Psalms 111 and 112, for they were willing, in the day of battle, that He rule over His enemies, when He crushed the kings and judged the nations of the world (Ps. 110:3–7).

Psalm 111 is an acrostic and topmost in it are the Lord's works. It is the assembly of the upright, also called a council, who praise the Lord for His great and powerful works, His glorious and majestic deeds.

Hallelujah.

I will extol the Lord with all my heart in the council of the upright and in the assembly. Great *are the works of the Lord*; they are pondered by all who delight in them. Glorious and majestic are *His deeds*, and His righteousness endures forever. He has caused_*His wonders* to be remembered; the Lord is gracious and compassionate. He provides food for those who fear Him. He remembers His covenant forever. He has shown His people the power of *His works*, giving them the lands of other nations. *The works of His hands* are faithful and just; all His precepts are trustworthy. They are steadfast forever and ever, done in faithfulness and uprightness. *He provided redemption for His people*; He ordained His covenant forever—holy and awesome is His name. The fear of the Lord is the beginning of wisdom; all who follow His precepts have good understanding. To Him belongs eternal praise (Ps. 111:1–10, emphasis is added).

When the assembled saints were in heaven and the Lord became King over all the earth, they shouted for joy saying, He subdued nations under us, peoples under our feet (Ps. 47:1–3). Now He has caused His wonders to be remembered. . . . He has shown His people the power of His works, giving them the lands of other nations (Ps. 111:4, 6).

Two times they mention His covenant, which He remembers, for at His coming He extends all the borders of Israel (Isa. 26:15). When their eyes see the King in His beauty they will view a land that stretches afar (Isa. 33:17). Fulfilling His covenant with Abraham, He now gives to His descendants all the land from the River of Egypt, the Wadi El-Arish, to the Euphrates. Their north border, extending to Hamath, will give them Lebanon, half of Syria and half of Iraq. The south border, beginning in lower Kuwait, extends westward to Ezion Gerber on the Red Sea, from where it will follow Brook of Egypt to the Great Sea. Their land will also include most of Saudi Arabia, all of Jordan and all of Gaza.

Psalm 112. The blessed man in this acrostic is topmost among those seated on thrones to judge. His horn will be lifted high in honor because of his generosity while on earth (A horn = a king Dan. 7:24).

Hallelujah.

Blessed is the man who fears the LORD, who finds great delight in His commandments. His children will be mighty in the land; the generation of the upright will be blessed. Wealth and riches are in his house, and his righteousness endures forever. Even in darkness light dawns for the upright, for the gracious and compassionate and righteous man. Good will come to him who is generous and lends freely, who conducts his affairs with justice. Surely he will never be shaken; a righteous man will be remembered forever. He will have no fear of bad news; his heart is steadfast, trusting in the LORD. His heart is secure, he will have no fear; in the end he will look in triumph on his foes. He has scattered abroad his gifts to the poor, his righteousness endures forever; his horn will be lifted high in honor. The wicked man will see and be vexed, he will gnash with his teeth and waste away; the longings of the wicked will come to nothing (Ps. 112:1–10).

The Lord, who will choose our inheritance, will reward everyone according to what each has done while on earth. This blessed man was generous with his gifts to the poor, to those God has chosen to be rich in faith and to inherit the kingdom, which He promised to those who love Him. Judgment without mercy will be shown to everyone who has not been merciful (James 2:5,13). In the end, this generous man will look in triumph on his foes. The wicked man, who had no delight in the Lord's commands, will see the exalted righteous man and be vexed, he will gnash his teeth and waste away.

The next group to offer thankful adoration to their King are the Jews. They, who have returned to the land, will sing the Egyptian *Halal,* Psalms 113–118. Previously, they chanted them at their feasts, as at the Passover. Psalm 113 and 114 are sung before the meal and Psalms 115–118 are sung after the meal. Likewise, Psalms 113 and 114 emphasize what took place before the Jews returned to the land and Psalms 115–118 tell of what took place after their return.

Psalm 113.

Hallelujah.

Praise, O servants of the Lord, praise the name of the LORD. Let the name of the LORD be praised, both now and forevermore. From the rising of the sun to the place where it sets, the name of the LORD is to be praised. The LORD is exalted over all the nations, His glory above the heavens. Who is like the LORD our God, the One who sits enthroned on high, who stoops down to look on the heavens and the earth. He raised the poor from the dust and lifts the needy from the ash heap; He seats them with princes, with the princes of their people. He settles the barren woman in her home as a happy mother of children (Ps. 113:1–9).

Hallelujah.

In this prophecy, the Israelites who returned to Zion to praise their King call on others in His presence to do the same. They request the Lord's servants, the resurrected great tribulation saints who serve the Lord day and night in His temple, to praise Him now and forevermore. Who is like the Lord our God, exalted over the nations, the One who sits enthroned on high, who stoops down and lifts the poor and needy from the dust (at the resurrection of the Church) and seats them (on thrones) with the princes of their people. He it is who settles barren Israel in her home (land) as a happy mother of children. Isaiah said, Sing, O barren woman, you who never bore a child; burst into song, shout for joy, you who were never in labor; because more are the children of the desolate woman than of her who has a husband. . . . The Lord will call you back as if you were a wife deserted and distressed in spirit—a wife who married young, only to be rejected, says your God. For a brief moment I abandoned you, but with deep compassion I will bring you back (Isa. 54:1, 6–7).

Psalm 114.

When Israel came out of Egypt, the house of Jacob from a people of foreign tongue, Judah became Gods sanctuary, Israel His dominion. The sea looked and fled, the Jordan turned back; the mountains skipped like rams, the hills like lambs. Why was it,

O sea, that you fled, O Jordan that you turned back, you mountains, that you skipped like rams, you hills, like lambs? Tremble, O earth, at the presence of the Lord, at the presence of the God of Jacob, who turned the rock into a pool, the hard rock into springs of water. Ps. 114:1–8)

This second song of the Egyptian *Halal,* also speaks of what took place before Israel entered the land. What took place is introduced by the question, Why was it, O sea, that you fled, O Jordan, that you turned back, you mountains, that you skipped like rams, you hills, like lambs? The Lord gained honor for Himself by the great power He displayed against the Egyptians at the Red Sea. The nations hear and tremble; terror and dread fall upon them (Ex. 15:14–16). And when all the Amorite kings west of the Jordan and all the Canaanite kings along the coast heard how the LORD dried up the Jordan before the Israelites until they had crossed over, their hearts melted and they no longer had the courage to face the Israelites (Josh. 5:1).

As for the trembling mountains and hills, Mount Sinai trembled violently before the Lord descended upon it (Ex. 19:18–20). Likewise, in the night of the Passover day, before the Lord descends to the earth as King, there will be a severe earthquake. No earthquake like it has ever occurred since man has been on earth, so tremendous was the quake (Rev. 16:18). Men will flee to caves in the rocks and to holes in the ground from dread of the LORD and the splendor of His majesty, when He rises to shake the earth (Isa. 2:19). When God makes the Lord head of the nations, people He did not know are subject to Him and obey Him. Foreigners cringe before Him. They all lose heart; they come trembling from their strongholds (Ps. 18:43–45).

Just as the Israelites sang the last four psalms of the Egyptian *Halal* after they ate the Passover, so also the events in these psalms take place after the Passover morning, and after the Lord has returned to Zion.

Psalm 115. We will give the beginning and the end of Psalms 115–116 and 118.

Not to us, O LORD, not to us but to your name be the glory, because of your love and faithfulness. Why do the nations say, Where is their God? Our God is in heaven; he does whatever pleases Him . . . (Ps. 115:1–3).

The highest heavens belong to the LORD, but the earth He has given to man. It is not the dead who praise the LORD, those who go down to silence; it is we who extol the LORD, both now and forevermore (Ps. 115:16–18).

Hallelujah.

Between these verses, it is the house of Israel and her priests who are to trust in the Lord, for it is He, the maker of the heavens and the earth, who will bless them—small and great alike.

Psalm 116.

I love the LORD, for he heard my voice; he heard my cry for mercy. Because he turned his ear to me, I will call upon him as long as I live . . . (Ps. 116:1–2).

I will sacrifice a thank offering to you and call on the name of the LORD. I will fulfill my vows to the LORD in the presence of all his people, in the courts of the house of the LORD—in your midst, O Jerusalem (Ps. 116:17–18).

Hallelujah.

In the verses omitted, this soul relates how he called on the Lord when in great need, when overcome by trouble and sorrow, and the Lord saved him. For the Lord's goodness to him, he will lift up the cup of salvation, call on the Lord, and fulfill his vows to the Lord in the presence of all His people.

Psalm 117. This is the third song that is sung after the meal and which takes place after they return to the land.

Praise the LORD, all you nations; exalt him, all you peoples. For great is his love toward us, and the faithfulness of the LORD endures forever (Ps. 117:1–2).

Hallelujah.

Psalm 118.

Give thanks to the LORD, for He is good; His love endures forever. Let Israel say: His love endures forever. Let the house of Aaron say: His love endures forever. Let those who fear the Lord say: His love endures forever (Ps. 118:1–4).

. . . O LORD, save us; O LORD, grant us success. Blessed is He who comes in the name of the LORD. From the house of the LORD we bless You. The LORD is God, and He has made His light shine upon us. With boughs in hand, join in the festal procession up to the horns of the altar. You are my God, and I will give You thanks; You are my God, and I will exalt You. Give thanks to the LORD, for He is good; His love endures forever (Ps. 118:25–29).

Between the opening and closing portions of Psalm 118, an Israelite tells how he, when surrounded by the nations, was in anguish. He called upon the Lord, his helper, who set Him free. All the nations surrounded me on every side, but in the name of the Lord I cut them off. They died quickly like burning thorns (vv. 10–12). The Lord is my strength and my song; He has become my salvation. Shouts of joy and victory resounded in the tents of the righteous (vv. 14–15). The Lord's right hand has done mighty things, and I will proclaim what He has done. Open for me the gates of the Lord, through which the righteous may enter. I will give You thanks, for You answered me; You have become my salvation (v. 21).

But the righteous may not enter the Lord's gates into His courts until they have been taught the precepts the Lord laid down; they are to be fully observed. A double blessing awaits those who walk according to His law, keep His statutes and seek Him with all their heart (Ps. 119:1–4). To them the gates will be opened. As they ascend the seven steps into His outer court and the eight steps into His inner court, they sing one of the fifteen Songs of the Ascents on each step (Ezek. 40:26, 31; Ps. 120–134). When they enter into the Kings presence, they sing the great *Hallel*, Psalms 135 and 136. Only the beginning and the end of them will be given.

Psalm 135.

Hallelujah.

Praise the name of the LORD; praise Him, you servants of the LORD, you who minister in the house of the LORD, in the courts of the house of our God. Praise the LORD, for the LORD is good; sing praise to His name, for that is pleasant. For the LORD has chosen Jacob to be His own, Israel to be His treasured possession . . . (Ps. 135:1–4).

O house of Israel, praise the LORD; O house of Aaron, praise the LORD; O house of Levi, praise the LORD; you who fear Him, praise the LORD. Praise be to the LORD from Zion, to Him who dwells in Jerusalem (Ps. 135:20–22).

Hallelujah.

More reasons are given to praise the Lord between the opening and closing portions of this psalm. The Lord is great; He does what pleases Him in the heavens, on the earth, and in the seas. He causes clouds to arise, sends lightning with the rain and winds from His storehouses. He struck down the firstborn in Egypt and sent signs and wonders against Pharaoh and his servants. He struck down many nations and mighty kings, giving their lands to Israel as an inheritance. He is greater than the idols of the nations.

Psalm 136.

Give thanks to the Lord, for He is good.

His love endures forever.

Give thanks to the God of gods.

His love endures forever.

Give thanks to the Lord of lords;

His love endures forever. (verses 1–3)

Give thanks to the God of heaven.

His love endures forever. (verse 26)

Psalms 135 and 136 are called the great *Hallel* because of the repeated response in this psalm by the congregation after a reason is given to do so by the cantor. The Lord's name, King of kings and Lord of lords, was on His robe and thigh when He came from heaven leading His armies (Rev. 19:16).

Between these calls to give Him thanks, they continue to do this for many reasons. For His great wonders and understanding when He made the heavens and spread out the earth upon the waters; for making the great lights, the sun, the moon, and the stars; for bringing Israel out of Egypt with a mighty hand after striking down the firstborn of Egypt; for dividing the Red Sea, to bring Israel through it and sweep Pharaoh and his army into it; for leading Israel through the desert; for striking down great nations and mighty king to give their lands as an inheritance to His people Israel; for remembering Israel in her low estate and freeing them from their enemies.

Israel's low estate will begin when the king of the ten nations invade Israel with 200,000,000 mounted troops (Rev. 9:13–16). Then Israel, the woman of Revelation 12:1–17, will flee Jerusalem to the wilderness for 1260 days. These nations will defile the temple, reduce Jerusalem to rubble and give the dead bodies of the Lord's servants and the saints to the birds and the beasts of the earth. Gods anger against Israel will burn like fire. In Psalm 79, an Israelite in Israel's low estate asks the Lord to pay back into the laps of our neighbors seven times the reproach they have hurled at You, O Lord. Then we Your people, the sheep of Your pasture, will praise You forever; from generation to generation we will recount Your praise (Psalm 79: 12–13). Israel is now recounting His praise in Psalm 136 and will continue to do from everlasting to everlasting.

Books 4 and 5 end with psalms that begin and end with Praise the Lord. These are Psalms 105 and 106 of Book 4 and Psalms 146–150 of Book 5. As stated previously, the words Praise the Lord, which should appear at the beginning of Psalm 105, are found at the end of Psalm 104. We will present the beginning and the ending of the long psalms.

Psalm 105.

Hallelujah.

Give thanks to the Lord, call on His name; make known among the nations what He has done. Sing to Him, sing praise to Him; tell of all His wonderful acts. Glory in His holy name; let the hearts of those who seek the Lord rejoice. Look to the Lord and His strength; seek His face always. (Ps. 105:1–4)

For He remembered His holy promise given to His servant Abraham. He brought out His people with rejoicing, His chosen ones with shouts of joy; He gave them the lands of the nations, and they fell heir to what others toiled for that they might keep His precepts and observe His laws. (Ps. 105:42–45)

Hallelujah.

The wonderful acts the Lord has done to give to Israel the lands of the nations is told between these portions. When Jacob was few in number, He brought famine on the land. He sent Joseph ahead of them into Egypt to teach his elders wisdom. Then Jacob entered Egypt and the Lord made His people too numerous for their foes. Their foes hated them. The Lord sent Moses and Aaron to perform miraculous signs in Egypt, because they rebelled against His word. To them He sent darkness, and turned their water into blood. He sent frogs, swarms of flies, gnats and hail, followed by locusts. He then struck down all the first born and brought Israel out laden with silver and gold. [cf. Ex. 3:21–22] He spread His cloud over them and gave them light at night. He gave them quail and bread from heaven and water like a river from the rock. For He remembered His holy promise to Abraham to give the lands of the nations to His people that they might observe His laws. The lands of the nations are now theirs and they are obeying His precepts.

Psalm 106.

Hallelujah.

Give thanks to the LORD, for He is good; His love endures forever. Who can proclaim the mighty acts of the LORD or fully declare His praise? Blessed are they who maintain justice, who constantly do what is right. Remember me, O LORD, when You show favor to Your people, come to my aid when You save them, that I may enjoy the prosperity of Your chosen ones, that I may share in the joy of Your nation and join Your inheritance in giving praise . . . (Ps. 106:1–5)

But He took note of their distress when He heard their cry; for their sake He remembered His covenant and out of great love He relented. He caused them to be pitied by all who held them captive. Save us, O LORD our God, and gather us from the nations, that we may give thanks to Your holy name and glory in Your praise. Praise be the LORD, the God of Israel, from everlasting to everlasting. Let all the people say, Amen! (Ps. 106:44–48)

Hallelujah.

In the long portion omitted, they tell how they sinned as their fathers did and how they defiled themselves by their deeds. The Lord was angry with His people and handed them over to the nations who ruled over them and oppressed them until He took note of their distress.

Psalm 146.

Hallelujah.

Praise the LORD, O my soul. I will praise the LORD all my life; I will sing praise to my God as long as I live . . . (Ps. 1461–2).

The LORD reigns forever, your God, O Zion, for all generations (Ps. 146:10).

Hallelujah.

The blessed, who put their trust and hope in the Lord, are presented between these quotes. They are the following: the oppressed, the hungry, the prisoners, the blind, those bowed down, the righteous, the alien, the fatherless, and the widow.

Psalm 147.

Hallelujah.

How good it is to sing praise to our God, how pleasant and fitting to praise Him . . . (Ps. 147:1).

He has revealed His Word to Jacob, His law and decrees to Israel. He has done this for no other nation; they do not know His laws (Ps. 147:19–20).

Hallelujah.

It is fitting to praise the Lord, as is done between the brief beginning and end of this psalm. He is praised for His greatness, His mighty power, and His understanding that has no limit. He builds up Jerusalem, gathers the exiles, heals the brokenhearted and binds up their wounds. He determines the number of stars and calls each by their name. He sustains the humble and casts the wicked to the ground. He covers the sky with clouds, supplies the rain for grass to grow, He provides food for the cattle and the young ravens when they call. He delights in those who fear Him, who hope in His unfailing Love. He strengthens the bars of Jerusalem's gates, blesses His people with peace and feeds them with the finest wheat. His command to the earth runs swiftly; He spreads the snow, scatters the frost and hurls down the hail. Who can withstand His icy blast? He sends breezes, melts them and waters flow.

Psalm 148.

Hallelujah.

Praise the LORD from the heavens, praise Him in the heights above. Praise Him, all His angels, praise Him all His heavenly hosts. Praise Him, sun and moon, praise Him all you shining stars. Praise Him, you highest heavens and you waters above the skies. Let them praise the name of the LORD, for He commanded and they were created. He set them in place forever and ever; He gave a decree that will never pass away. *Praise the LORD from the earth*, you great sea creatures and all ocean depths, lightning and hail, snow and clouds, stormy winds that do His bidding, you mountains and all hills, fruit trees and all cedars, wild animals and all cattle, small creatures and flying birds, kings of the earth and all nations, you princes and all rulers on earth, young men and maidens, old men and children. Let them praise the name of the LORD, for His name alone is exalted; His splendor is above the earth and the heavens. He has raised up for His people a horn, the praise of all His saints, of Israel, the people close to His heart. (Ps. 148:1–14, emphasis added).

Hallelujah.

When God installs His King on Zions holy hill, all the heavenly hosts will praise the Lord. The sun and moon will do the same: The moon will shine like the sun and the sun will be seven times brighter (Isa. 30:26). The sea creatures will praise Him as will lightning, hail and stormy wind that do His bidding.

Mountains and hills that are brought low will praise Him as do the fruitful trees. Wild animals do the same: The wolf will live with the lamb, the leopard with the goat and the lion with the calf; they will neither harm or destroy in all His holy mountain (Isa. 11:6–9). All the rulers on earth will praise Him as will men, maidens and children. All do this because God raised up a horn for Israel, a people close to His heart.

Psalm 149.

Hallelujah.

Sing to the LORD a new song, His praise in the assembly of the saints. Let Israel rejoice in their Maker; let the people of Zion be glad in their King. Let them praise His name with dancing and make music to Him with tambourine and harp. For the LORD takes delight in His people; He crowns the humble with salvation. Let the saints rejoice in this honor and sing for joy on their beds. May the praise of God be in their mouths and a double edged sword in their hands, to inflict vengeance on the nations and punishment on the peoples, to bind their kings with fetters, their nobles with shackles of iron, to carry out the sentence written against them. This is the glory of all His saints. (Ps. 149:1–9)

Hallelujah.

This is the sentence written against the nations: For the nation or kingdom that will not serve You will perish; it will be utterly ruined (Isa. 60:12). In Psalm 101:8, this also is written: Every morning I will put to silence all the wicked in the land; I will cut off every evildoer from the city of the LORD. If the Lord does this in Israel, will not those seated on thrones judging the nations do the same. And this is the word of the Lord concerning Israel: On the day, when all the nations of the earth are gathered against her. . . . I will make the leaders of Jacob like a firepot in a woodpile, like a flaming torch among sheaves. They will consume right and left all the surrounding peoples. . . . On that day, the LORD will shield those who live in Jerusalem, so that the feeblest among them will be like David, and the house of David will be like God, like the Angel of the Lord going before them (Zech. 12:1–8). This is the glory of all His saints. The double-edged sword in their hand is the name of the LORD (Ps. 118:10–12).

Psalm 150.

Hallelujah.

Praise God in His sanctuary; praise Him in His mighty heavens. Praise Him for His acts of power; praise Him for His surpassing greatness. Praise Him with the sounding of the trumpet, praise Him with the harp and lyre, praise Him with tambourine and dancing, praise Him with the strings and flute, praise Him with the clash of cymbals, praise Him with resounding cymbals. Let everything that has breath praise the LORD (Ps. 150:1–5).

Hallelujah.

The day is soon to come, when mankind will recognize the surpassing greatness of the acts of the Lord's power, majesty, and love, and will praise Him for what He has done. The removal of the wicked from the earth, which He will begin to do in the night before He comes as King, will continue to be done through the days of His reign from Zion. The coming days, when He dwells with men, are a preparation for the days of eternity, when God will dwell with men. Today, the day when the Holy Spirit dwells with the believers, is nearly over. More than 1900 years have passed since Jesus said, Behold, I am coming soon! Amen. Come, Lord Jesus (Rev. 22:7, 20).

Bibliography
Bibles

New International Version - NIV, Large Print Study Bible, 10th Anniversary Edition, 1955 by

The Zondervan Publishing House, Grand Rapids, MI 49530, USA.

New King James Version - NKJV, 1982 by Thomas Nelson Inc., Nashville, Tennessee.

The MacArthur Study Bible - NKJV. 1997 by Word Publishing, Nashville, TN., 37214

The New English Bible, 1970 by Oxford University Press - Cambridge University Press, USA.

Revised Standard Version - RSV, 1952 by Thomas Nelson and Sons, New York.

New American Standard Translation. 1978 - The Ryrie Study Bible by Moody Press, Chicago, IL.

The Living Bible (Paraphrased), 1971 by Tyndale House Publishers, Wheaton, IL.

Life Application Study Bible, 1996 by Tyndale House Publishers, Inc., Wheaton, IL.

The Septuagint Bible, 1954 by The Falcon Wing press.

The New Jerusalem Bible, 1985 by Doubleday and Company, Inc., Garden City, N.Y.

To order additional copies of

TWO PLOTS AGAINST THE LORD

Have your credit card ready and call:

1-877-421-READ (7323)

or please visit our web site at
www.pleasantword.com

Also available at: www.amazon.com

Printed in the United States
1293100005B/244-399